Take It to Your Seat Centers

COMMON CORE Math 5

Using the Centers

The 12 centers in this book provide hands-on practice to help students master standards-based mathematics skills. It is important to teach each skill and to model the use of each center before asking students to do the tasks independently. The centers are self-contained and portable. Students can work at a desk, at a table, or on a rug, and they can use the centers as often as needed.

Why Use Centers?

- Centers are a motivating way for students to practice important skills.

- They provide for differentiated instruction.

- They appeal especially to kinesthetic and visual learners.

- They are ready to use whenever instruction or practice in the target skill is indicated.

Before Using Centers

You and your students will enjoy using centers more if you think through logistical considerations. Here are a few questions to resolve ahead of time:

- Will students select a center, or will you assign the centers and use them as a skill assessment tool?

- Will there be a specific block of time for centers, or will the centers be used by students throughout the day as they complete other work?

- Where will you place the centers for easy access by students?

- What procedure will students use when they need help with the center tasks?

- Will students use the answer key to check their own work?

- How will you use the center checklist to track completion of the centers?

Introducing the Centers

Use the teacher instructions page and the student directions on the center's cover page to teach or review the skill. Show students the pieces of the center and model how to use them as you read each step of the directions.

If you find some of the skills too challenging for your students, you may want to use one or more of the centers only for group work, or you might use the center several times with a group before assigning it for independent use. You also have the option of assigning only part of a center for independent work.

Recording Progress

Use the center checklist (page 4) to record both the date when a student completes each center and the student's skill level at that point.

Making the Centers

Included for Each Center

(A) Student directions/cover page

(B) Task cards and mat(s)

(C) Reproducible activity

(D) Answer key

Materials Needed

- Folders with inside pockets

- Small envelopes or self-closing plastic bags (for storing task cards)

- Pencils or marking pens (for labeling envelopes)

- Scissors

- Double-sided tape (for attaching the cover page to the front of the folder)

- Laminating equipment

How to Assemble and Store

1. Tape the center's cover page to the front of the folder.

2. Place reproduced activity pages and a supply of scratch paper in the left-hand pocket of the folder.

3. Laminate mats and task cards.

4. Cut apart the task cards and put them in a labeled envelope or self-closing plastic bag. Place the mats and task cards in the right-hand pocket of the folder. If you want the centers to be self-checking, include the answer key in the folder.

5. Store prepared centers in a file box or a crate.

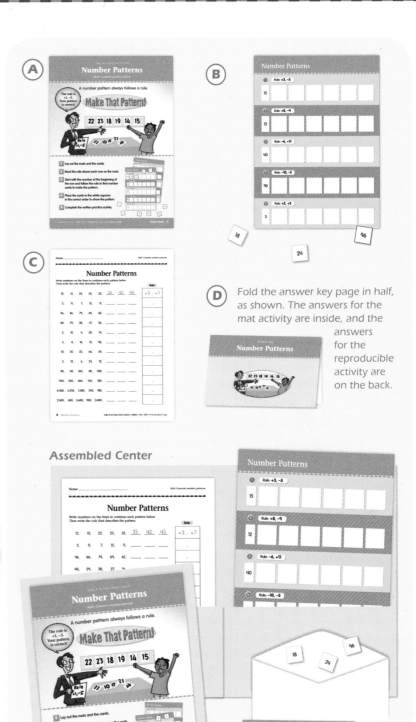

(D) Fold the answer key page in half, as shown. The answers for the mat activity are inside, and the answers for the reproducible activity are on the back.

Assembled Center

Student _____

Center Checklist

Center / Skill	Skill Level	Date
1. Number Patterns Generate number patterns that follow given rules		
2. Prime or Composite? Identify prime and composite numbers		
3. Compare Decimals Compare decimals (to thousandths), using greater than, less than, and equal to symbols		
4. Computation Speed Drill Build fluency with multiplication and division facts from 6 through 12		
5. Add and Subtract Fractions Add and subtract fractions with unlike denominators		
6. Real-World Word Problems Use the four operations to solve real-world, multistep word problems		
7. Equivalent Measurements Convert units of length and capacity within measurement systems (U.S. customary and metric)		
8. Plot It! Display and interpret data on a line plot		
9. Measures of Center Find the range, mean, median, and mode in sets of numbers		
10. Volume Measure the volume of rectangular prisms by counting unit cubes and by applying the formula $V = l \times w \times h$		
11. What Is the Chance? Compute probability for simple chance events		
12. Math Terms Extend understanding of math vocabulary		

Take It to Your Seat Centers—Math • EMC 3075 • © Evan-Moor Corp.

Number Patterns

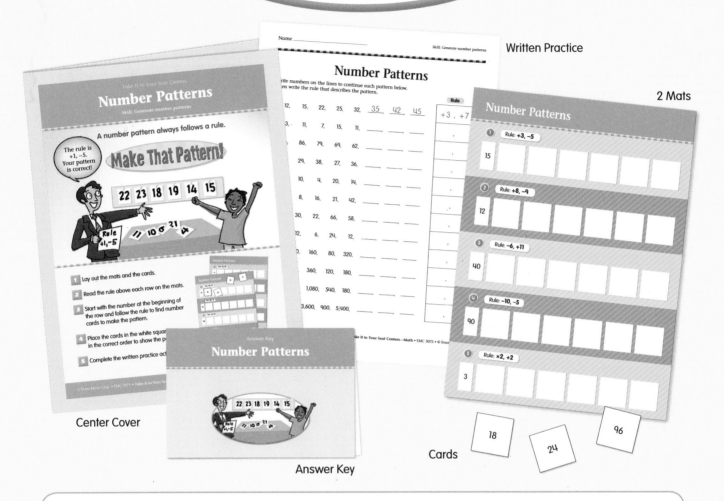

Center Cover

Answer Key

Cards

Written Practice

2 Mats

Skill: Generate number patterns that follow given rules

Steps to Follow

1. **Prepare the center.** (See page 3.)

2. **Introduce the center.** State the goal. Say: *You will read each rule on the mats and place number cards in the squares to create the pattern.*

3. **Teach the skill.** Demonstrate how to use the center with individual students or small groups.

4. **Practice the skill.** Have students use the center independently or with a partner.

Contents

Number Patterns

Write numbers on the lines to continue each pattern below.
Then write the rule that describes the pattern.

								Rule
12,	15,	22,	25,	32,	_35_,	_42_,	_45_	+3 , +7
3,	11,	7,	15,	11,	____,	____,	____	,
96,	86,	79,	69,	62,	____,	____,	____	,
40,	29,	38,	27,	36,	____,	____,	____	,
2,	10,	4,	20,	14,	____,	____,	____	,
3,	8,	16,	21,	42,	____,	____,	____	,
10,	30,	22,	66,	58,	____,	____,	____	,
3,	12,	6,	24,	12,	____,	____,	____	,
80,	40,	160,	80,	320,	____,	____,	____	,
900,	300,	360,	120,	180,	____,	____,	____	,
6,480,	3,240,	1,080,	540,	180,	____,	____,	____	,
2,400,	600,	3,600,	900,	5,400,	____,	____,	____	,

Number Patterns

Skill: Generate number patterns

A number pattern always follows a rule.

1. Lay out the mats and the cards.

2. Read the rule above each row on the mats.

3. Start with the number at the beginning of the row and follow the rule to find number cards to make the pattern.

4. Place the cards in the white squares in the correct order to show the pattern.

5. Complete the written practice activity.

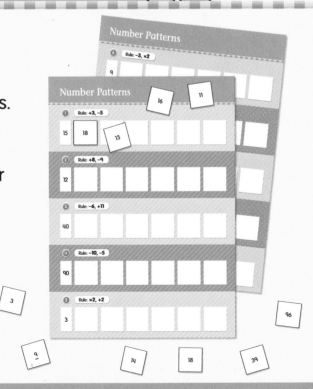

Number Patterns

Answer Key

(fold)

Written Practice

Number Patterns

Write numbers on the lines to continue each pattern below.
Then write the rule that describes the pattern.

								Rule
12,	15,	22,	25,	32,	35	42	45	+ 3 , +7
3,	11,	7,	15,	11,	19	15	23	+8 , –4
96,	86,	79,	69,	62,	52	45	35	–10 , –7
40,	29,	38,	27,	36,	25	34	23	–11 , +9
2,	10,	4,	20,	14,	70	64	320	×5 , –6
3,	8,	16,	21,	42,	47	94	99	+5 , ×2
10,	30,	22,	66,	58,	174	166	498	×3 , –8
3,	12,	6,	24,	12,	48	24	96	×4 , ÷2
80,	40,	160,	80,	320,	160	640	320	÷2 , ×4
900,	300,	360,	120,	180,	60	120	40	÷3 , +60
6,480,	3,240,	1,080,	540,	180,	90	30	15	÷2 , ÷3
2,400,	600,	3,600,	900,	5,400,	1,350	8,100	2,025	÷4 , ×6

Answer Key
Number Patterns

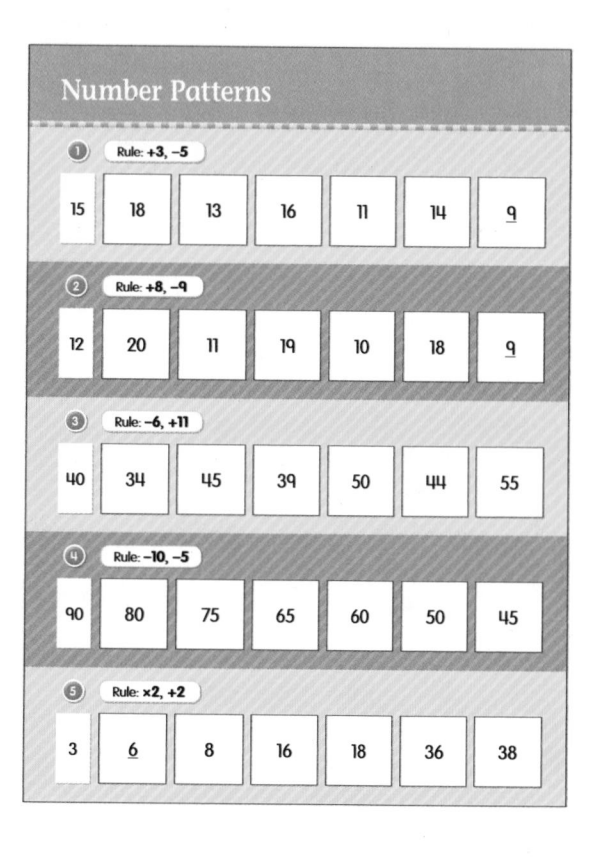

Number Patterns

1 Rule: +3, −5
| 15 | 18 | 13 | 16 | 11 | 14 | <u>9</u> |

2 Rule: +8, −9
| 12 | 20 | 11 | 19 | 10 | 18 | <u>9</u> |

3 Rule: −6, +11
| 40 | 34 | 45 | 39 | 50 | 44 | 55 |

4 Rule: −10, −5
| 90 | 80 | 75 | 65 | 60 | 50 | 45 |

5 Rule: ×2, +2
| 3 | <u>6</u> | 8 | 16 | 18 | 36 | 38 |

Number Patterns

6 Rule: −3, ×2
| 9 | <u>6</u> | 12 | <u>9</u> | 18 | 15 | 30 |

7 Rule: ×3, ×1
| 1 | 3 | 3 | <u>9</u> | <u>9</u> | 27 | 27 |

8 Rule: −8, ÷2
| 80 | 72 | 36 | 28 | 14 | <u>6</u> | 3 |

9 Rule: ×6, ÷3
| 4 | 24 | 8 | 48 | 16 | 96 | 32 |

10 Rule: ÷4, ÷1
| 256 | 64 | 64 | 16 | 16 | 4 | 4 |

Number Patterns

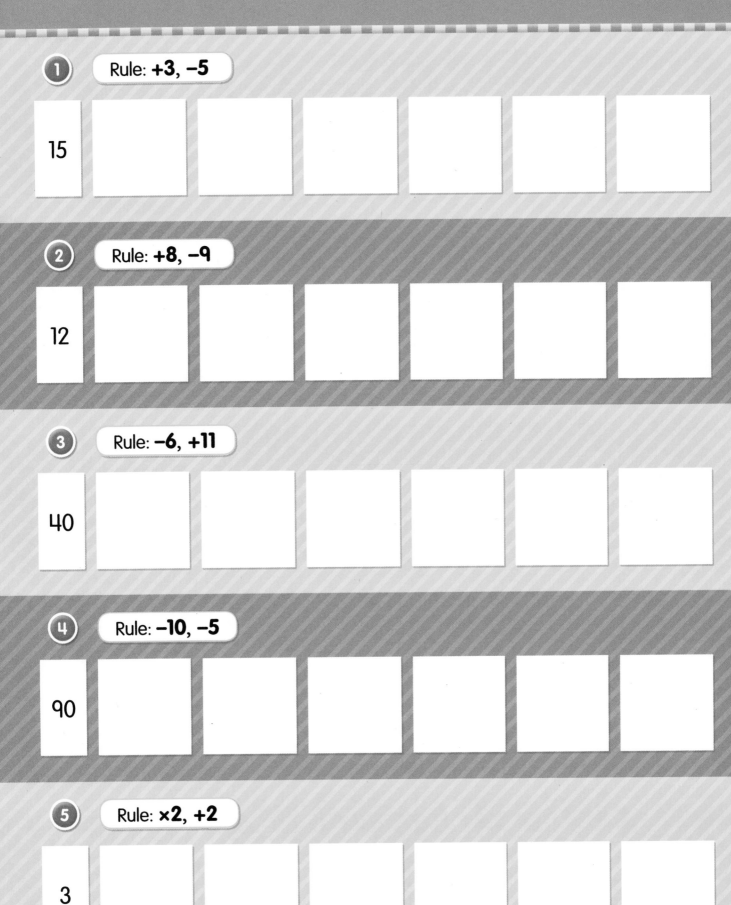

1 Rule: **+3, −5**

15						

2 Rule: **+8, −9**

12						

3 Rule: **−6, +11**

40						

4 Rule: **−10, −5**

90						

5 Rule: **×2, +2**

3						

Number Patterns

6 Rule: **−3, ×2**

9						

7 Rule: **×3, ×1**

1						

8 Rule: **−8, ÷2**

80						

9 Rule: **×6, ÷3**

4						

10 Rule: **÷4, ÷1**

256					

3	3	3	4	4	<u>6</u>	<u>6</u>
<u>6</u>	8	8	8	<u>9</u>	<u>9</u>	<u>9</u>
<u>9</u>	<u>9</u>	10	11	11	12	13
14	14	15	16	16	16	16
16	18	18	18	18	19	20
24	27	27	28	30	32	34
36	36	37	38	39	44	45
45	48	50	50	55	60	63
64	64	65	72	75	80	96

Number Patterns	Number Patterns	Number Patterns	Number Patterns	Number Patterns	Number Patterns	Number Patterns
EMC 3075 © Evan-Moor Corp.	EMC 3075 © Evan-Moor Corp.	EMC 3075 © Evan-Moor Corp.	EMC 3075 © Evan-Moor Corp.	EMC 3075 © Evan-Moor Corp.	EMC 3075 © Evan-Moor Corp.	EMC 3075 © Evan-Moor Corp.
Number Patterns	Number Patterns	Number Patterns	Number Patterns	Number Patterns	Number Patterns	Number Patterns
EMC 3075 © Evan-Moor Corp.	EMC 3075 © Evan-Moor Corp.	EMC 3075 © Evan-Moor Corp.	EMC 3075 © Evan-Moor Corp.	EMC 3075 © Evan-Moor Corp.	EMC 3075 © Evan-Moor Corp.	EMC 3075 © Evan-Moor Corp.
Number Patterns	Number Patterns	Number Patterns	Number Patterns	Number Patterns	Number Patterns	Number Patterns
EMC 3075 © Evan-Moor Corp.	EMC 3075 © Evan-Moor Corp.	EMC 3075 © Evan-Moor Corp.	EMC 3075 © Evan-Moor Corp.	EMC 3075 © Evan-Moor Corp.	EMC 3075 © Evan-Moor Corp.	EMC 3075 © Evan-Moor Corp.
Number Patterns	Number Patterns	Number Patterns	Number Patterns	Number Patterns	Number Patterns	Number Patterns
EMC 3075 © Evan-Moor Corp.	EMC 3075 © Evan-Moor Corp.	EMC 3075 © Evan-Moor Corp.	EMC 3075 © Evan-Moor Corp.	EMC 3075 © Evan-Moor Corp.	EMC 3075 © Evan-Moor Corp.	EMC 3075 © Evan-Moor Corp.
Number Patterns	Number Patterns	Number Patterns	Number Patterns	Number Patterns	Number Patterns	Number Patterns
EMC 3075 © Evan-Moor Corp.	EMC 3075 © Evan-Moor Corp.	EMC 3075 © Evan-Moor Corp.	EMC 3075 © Evan-Moor Corp.	EMC 3075 © Evan-Moor Corp.	EMC 3075 © Evan-Moor Corp.	EMC 3075 © Evan-Moor Corp.
Number Patterns	Number Patterns	Number Patterns	Number Patterns	Number Patterns	Number Patterns	Number Patterns
EMC 3075 © Evan-Moor Corp.	EMC 3075 © Evan-Moor Corp.	EMC 3075 © Evan-Moor Corp.	EMC 3075 © Evan-Moor Corp.	EMC 3075 © Evan-Moor Corp.	EMC 3075 © Evan-Moor Corp.	EMC 3075 © Evan-Moor Corp.
Number Patterns	Number Patterns	Number Patterns	Number Patterns	Number Patterns	Number Patterns	Number Patterns
EMC 3075 © Evan-Moor Corp.	EMC 3075 © Evan-Moor Corp.	EMC 3075 © Evan-Moor Corp.	EMC 3075 © Evan-Moor Corp.	EMC 3075 © Evan-Moor Corp.	EMC 3075 © Evan-Moor Corp.	EMC 3075 © Evan-Moor Corp.
Number Patterns	Number Patterns	Number Patterns	Number Patterns	Number Patterns	Number Patterns	Number Patterns
EMC 3075 © Evan-Moor Corp.	EMC 3075 © Evan-Moor Corp.	EMC 3075 © Evan-Moor Corp.	EMC 3075 © Evan-Moor Corp.	EMC 3075 © Evan-Moor Corp.	EMC 3075 © Evan-Moor Corp.	EMC 3075 © Evan-Moor Corp.
Number Patterns	Number Patterns	Number Patterns	Number Patterns	Number Patterns	Number Patterns	Number Patterns
EMC 3075 © Evan-Moor Corp.	EMC 3075 © Evan-Moor Corp.	EMC 3075 © Evan-Moor Corp.	EMC 3075 © Evan-Moor Corp.	EMC 3075 © Evan-Moor Corp.	EMC 3075 © Evan-Moor Corp.	EMC 3075 © Evan-Moor Corp.

Prime or Composite?

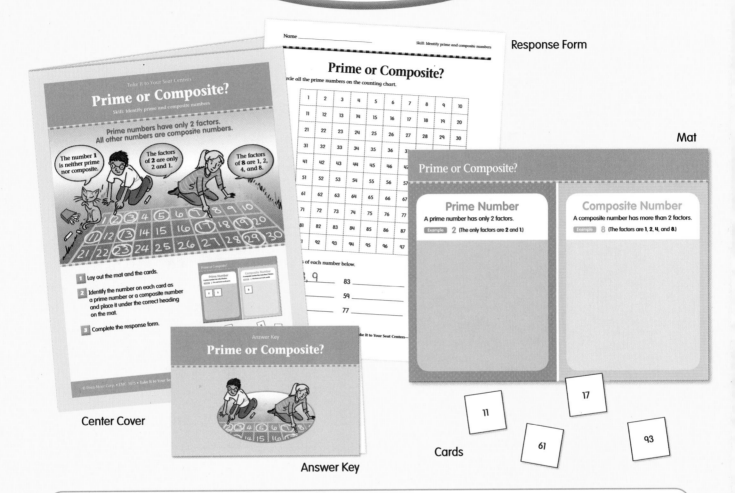

Response Form

Mat

Center Cover

Answer Key

Cards

Skill: Identify prime and composite numbers

Steps to Follow

1. **Prepare the center.** (See page 3.)

2. **Introduce the center.** State the goal. Say: *You will place number cards on the mat to show whether each number is prime or composite.*

3. **Teach the skill.** Demonstrate how to use the center with individual students or small groups.

4. **Practice the skill.** Have students use the center independently or with a partner.

Contents

Prime or Composite?

Circle all the prime numbers on the counting chart.

1	2	3	4	5	6	7	8	9	10
11	12	13	14	15	16	17	18	19	20
21	22	23	24	25	26	27	28	29	30
31	32	33	34	35	36	37	38	39	40
41	42	43	44	45	46	47	48	49	50
51	52	53	54	55	56	57	58	59	60
61	62	63	64	65	66	67	68	69	70
71	72	73	74	75	76	77	78	79	80
81	82	83	84	85	86	87	88	89	90
91	92	93	94	95	96	97	98	99	100

List the factors of each number below.

9 _1, 3, 9_   83 _____   47 _____

27 _____   59 _____   33 _____

13 _____   77 _____   69 _____

Take It to Your Seat Centers—Math • EMC 3075 • © Evan-Moor Corp.

Prime or Composite?

Skill: Identify prime and composite numbers

1. Lay out the mat and the cards.

2. Identify the number on each card as a prime number or a composite number and place it under the correct heading on the mat.

3. Complete the response form.

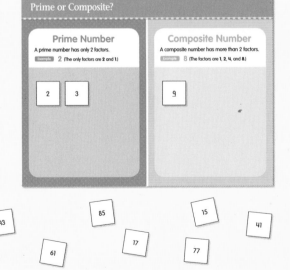

¿ətisodmoƆ ɹo əmirꓕ

Answer Key

(fold)

Response Form

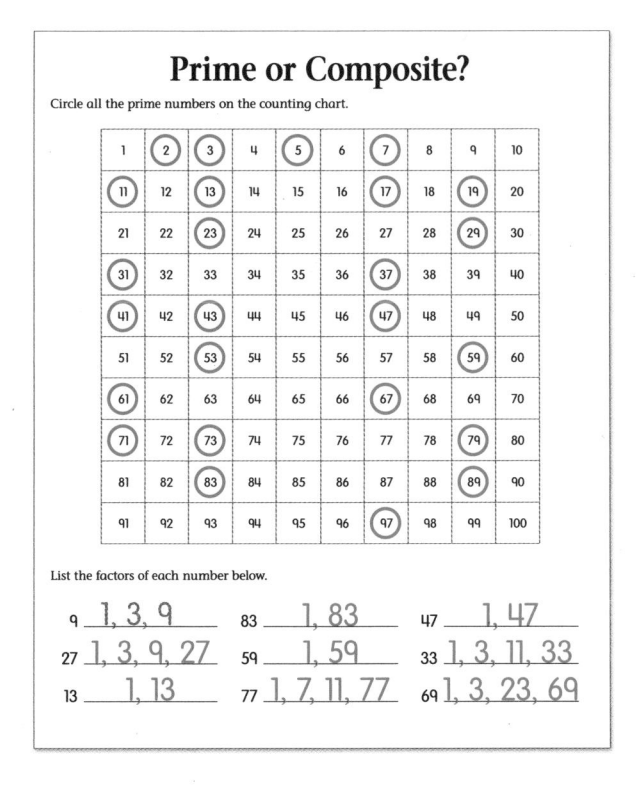

Prime or Composite?

Circle all the prime numbers on the counting chart.

1	(2)	(3)	4	(5)	6	(7)	8	9	10
(11)	12	(13)	14	15	16	(17)	18	(19)	20
21	22	(23)	24	25	26	27	28	(29)	30
(31)	32	33	34	35	36	(37)	38	39	40
(41)	42	(43)	44	45	46	(47)	48	49	50
51	52	(53)	54	55	56	57	58	(59)	60
(61)	62	63	64	65	66	(67)	68	69	70
(71)	72	(73)	74	75	76	77	78	(79)	80
81	82	(83)	84	85	86	87	88	(89)	90
91	92	93	94	95	96	(97)	98	99	100

List the factors of each number below.

9 __1, 3, 9__ 83 __1, 83__ 47 __1, 47__

27 __1, 3, 9, 27__ 59 __1, 59__ 33 __1, 3, 11, 33__

13 __1, 13__ 77 __1, 7, 11, 77__ 69 __1, 3, 23, 69__

Prime or Composite?

Prime or Composite?

Prime Number
A prime number has only 2 factors.

Example 2 (The only factors are **2** and **1**.)

2	3	5	7
11	13	17	19
23	29	31	37
41	43	47	53
59	61	67	71
73	79	83	89
97			

Composite Number
A composite number has more than 2 factors.

Example 8 (The factors are **1**, **2**, **4**, and **8**.)

9	15	21	25
27	33	35	39
45	49	51	55
57	63	65	69
75	77	81	85
87	91	93	95
99			

Prime or Composite?

Prime Number

A prime number has only 2 factors.

Example   2   (The only factors are **2** and **1**.)

Composite Number

A composite number has more than 2 factors.

Example   8   (The factors are **1**, **2**, **4**, and **8**.)

2	3	5	7	9	11	13
15	17	19	21	23	25	27
29	31	33	35	37	39	41
43	45	47	49	51	53	55
57	59	61	63	65	67	69
71	73	75	77	79	81	83
85	87	89	91	93	95	97
99						

Prime or Composite?

EMC 3075

© Evan-Moor Corp.

Prime or Composite?

EMC 3075

© Evan-Moor Corp.

Prime or Composite?

EMC 3075

© Evan-Moor Corp.

Prime or Composite?

EMC 3075

© Evan-Moor Corp.

Prime or Composite?

EMC 3075

© Evan-Moor Corp.

Prime or Composite?

EMC 3075

© Evan-Moor Corp.

Prime or Composite?

EMC 3075

© Evan-Moor Corp.

Prime or Composite?

EMC 3075

© Evan-Moor Corp.

Prime or Composite?

EMC 3075

© Evan-Moor Corp.

Prime or Composite?

EMC 3075

© Evan-Moor Corp.

Prime or Composite?

EMC 3075

© Evan-Moor Corp.

Prime or Composite?

EMC 3075

© Evan-Moor Corp.

Prime or Composite?

EMC 3075

© Evan-Moor Corp.

Prime or Composite?

EMC 3075

© Evan-Moor Corp.

Prime or Composite?

EMC 3075

© Evan-Moor Corp.

Prime or Composite?

EMC 3075

© Evan-Moor Corp.

Prime or Composite?

EMC 3075

© Evan-Moor Corp.

Prime or Composite?

EMC 3075

© Evan-Moor Corp.

Prime or Composite?

EMC 3075

© Evan-Moor Corp.

Prime or Composite?

EMC 3075

© Evan-Moor Corp.

Prime or Composite?

EMC 3075

© Evan-Moor Corp.

Prime or Composite?

EMC 3075

© Evan-Moor Corp.

Prime or Composite?

EMC 3075

© Evan-Moor Corp.

Prime or Composite?

EMC 3075

© Evan-Moor Corp.

Prime or Composite?

EMC 3075

© Evan-Moor Corp.

Prime or Composite?

EMC 3075

© Evan-Moor Corp.

Prime or Composite?

EMC 3075

© Evan-Moor Corp.

Prime or Composite?

EMC 3075

© Evan-Moor Corp.

Prime or Composite?

EMC 3075

© Evan-Moor Corp.

Prime or Composite?

EMC 3075

© Evan-Moor Corp.

Prime or Composite?

EMC 3075

© Evan-Moor Corp.

Prime or Composite?

EMC 3075

© Evan-Moor Corp.

Prime or Composite?

EMC 3075

© Evan-Moor Corp.

Prime or Composite?

EMC 3075

© Evan-Moor Corp.

Prime or Composite?

EMC 3075

© Evan-Moor Corp.

Prime or Composite?

EMC 3075

© Evan-Moor Corp.

Prime or Composite?

EMC 3075

© Evan-Moor Corp.

Prime or Composite?

EMC 3075

© Evan-Moor Corp.

Prime or Composite?

EMC 3075

© Evan-Moor Corp.

Prime or Composite?

EMC 3075

© Evan-Moor Corp.

Prime or Composite?

EMC 3075

© Evan-Moor Corp.

Prime or Composite?

EMC 3075

© Evan-Moor Corp.

Prime or Composite?

EMC 3075

© Evan-Moor Corp.

Prime or Composite?

EMC 3075

© Evan-Moor Corp.

Prime or Composite?

EMC 3075

© Evan-Moor Corp.

Prime or Composite?

EMC 3075

© Evan-Moor Corp.

Prime or Composite?

EMC 3075

© Evan-Moor Corp.

Prime or Composite?

EMC 3075

© Evan-Moor Corp.

Prime or Composite?

EMC 3075

© Evan-Moor Corp.

Prime or Composite?

EMC 3075

© Evan-Moor Corp.

Compare Decimals

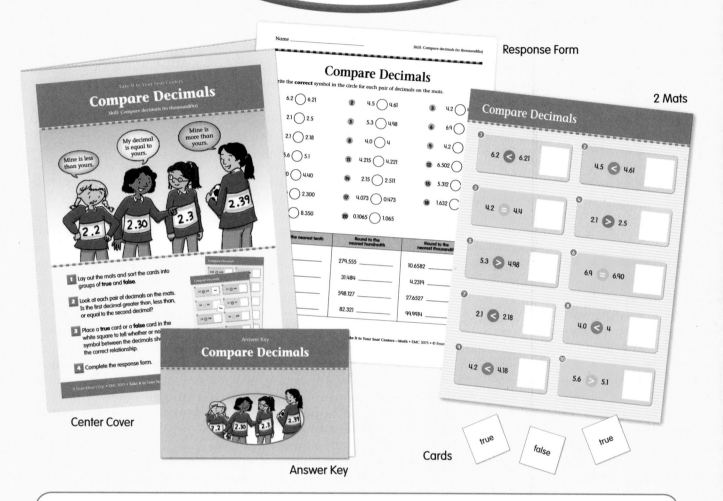

Response Form

2 Mats

Center Cover

Answer Key

Cards

Skill: Compare decimals (to thousandths), using greater than, less than, and equal to symbols

Steps to Follow

1. **Prepare the center.** (See page 3.)

2. **Introduce the center.** State the goal. Say: *You will compare each set of decimals on the mats and tell whether or not the symbol between them shows the correct relationship.*

3. **Teach the skill.** Demonstrate how to use the center with individual students or small groups.

4. **Practice the skill.** Have students use the center independently or with a partner.

Contents

Name ______________________

Skill: Compare decimals (to thousandths)

Compare Decimals

Write the **correct** symbol in the circle for each pair of decimals on the mats.

1. 6.2 ◯ 6.21
2. 4.5 ◯ 4.61
3. 4.2 ◯ 4.4
4. 2.1 ◯ 2.5
5. 5.3 ◯ 4.98
6. 6.9 ◯ 6.90
7. 2.1 ◯ 2.18
8. 4.0 ◯ 4
9. 4.2 ◯ 4.18
10. 5.6 ◯ 5.1
11. 4.215 ◯ 4.221
12. 6.502 ◯ 6.501
13. 4.20 ◯ 4.40
14. 2.15 ◯ 2.511
15. 5.312 ◯ 4.921
16. 2.30 ◯ 2.300
17. 4.073 ◯ 0.473
18. 1.632 ◯ 6.32
19. 8.35 ◯ 8.350
20. 0.1065 ◯ 1.065

Round to the nearest tenth	Round to the nearest hundredth	Round to the nearest thousandth
5.67 ________	279.555 ________	10.6582 ________
31.42 ________	31.484 ________	4.2319 ________
80.54 ________	598.127 ________	27.6527 ________
126.98 ________	82.321 ________	99.9914 ________

Compare Decimals

Skill: Compare decimals (to thousandths)

1 Lay out the mats and sort the cards into groups of **true** and **false**.

2 Look at each pair of decimals on the mats. Is the first decimal greater than, less than, or equal to the second decimal?

3 Place a **true** card or a **false** card in the white square to tell whether or not the symbol between the decimals shows the correct relationship.

4 Complete the response form.

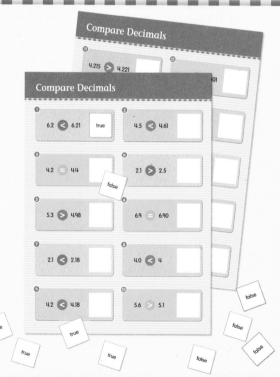

Compare Decimals

Write the **correct** symbol in the circle for each pair of decimals on the mats.

1 6.2 $>$ 6.21	2 4.5 $<$ 4.61	3 4.2 $>$ 4.4
4 2.1 $>$ .25	5 5.3 $<$ 4.98	6 6.9 $=$ 6.90
7 2.1 $>$ .218	8 4.0 $=$ 4	9 4.2 $>$ 4.18
10 5.6 $>$ 5.1	11 4.215 $>$ 4.221	12 6.502 $<$ 6.501
13 4.20 $>$ 4.40	14 2.15 $>$ 2.511	15 5.312 $<$ 4.921
16 2.30 $=$ 2.300	17 4.073 $<$ 0.473	18 1.632 $>$ 6.32
19 8.35 $=$ 8.350	20 0.1065 $<$ 1.065	

Round to the nearest tenth		Round to the nearest hundredth		Round to the nearest thousandth	
5.67	5.7	279.555	279.56	10.6582	10.658
31.42	31.4	31.484	31.48	4.2319	4.232
80.54	80.5	598.127	598.13	27.6527	27.653
126.98	127.0	82.321	82.32	99.9914	99.991

Response Form

(fold)

Answer Key

Compare Decimals

Answer Key

Compare Decimals

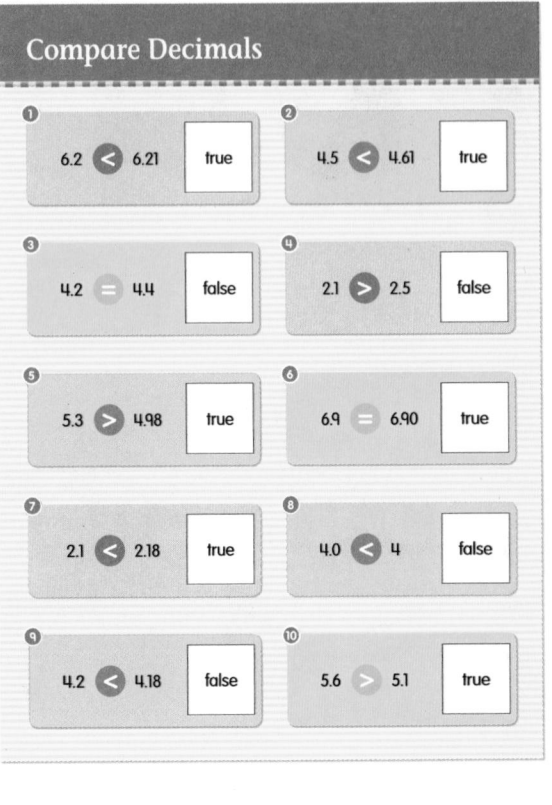

Compare Decimals

① 6.2 < 6.21 | true

② 4.5 < 4.61 | true

③ 4.2 = 4.4 | false

④ 2.1 > 2.5 | false

⑤ 5.3 > 4.98 | true

⑥ 6.9 = 6.90 | true

⑦ 2.1 < 2.18 | true

⑧ 4.0 < 4 | false

⑨ 4.2 < 4.18 | false

⑩ 5.6 > 5.1 | true

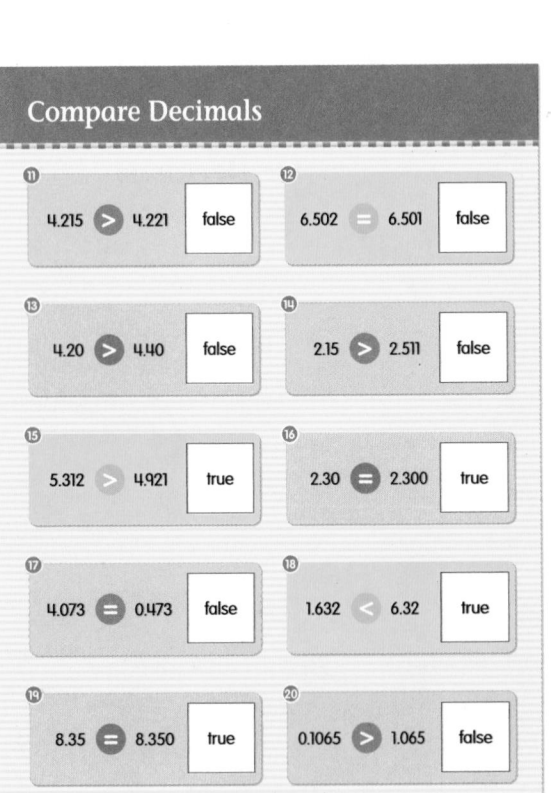

Compare Decimals

⑪ 4.215 > 4.221 | false

⑫ 6.502 = 6.501 | false

⑬ 4.20 > 4.40 | false

⑭ 2.15 > 2.511 | false

⑮ 5.312 > 4.921 | true

⑯ 2.30 = 2.300 | true

⑰ 4.073 = 0.473 | false

⑱ 1.632 < 6.32 | true

⑲ 8.35 = 8.350 | true

⑳ 0.1065 > 1.065 | false

Compare Decimals

1   6.2 < 6.21

2   4.5 < 4.61

3   4.2 = 4.4

4   2.1 > 2.5

5   5.3 > 4.98

6   6.9 = 6.90

7   2.1 < 2.18

8   4.0 < 4

9   4.2 < 4.18

10   5.6 > 5.1

Compare Decimals

11   4.215   **>**   4.221

12   6.502   **=**   6.501

13   4.20   **>**   4.40

14   2.15   **>**   2.511

15   5.312   **>**   4.921

16   2.30   **=**   2.300

17   4.073   **=**   0.473

18   1.632   **<**   6.32

19   8.35   **=**   8.350

20   0.1065   **>**   1.065

true	true	true	true	true
true	true	true	true	true
true	true	true	true	true
true	true	true	true	true
false	false	false	false	false
false	false	false	false	false
false	false	false	false	false
false	false	false	false	false

Compare Decimals	Compare Decimals	Compare Decimals	Compare Decimals	Compare Decimals
EMC 3075 © Evan-Moor Corp.	EMC 3075 © Evan-Moor Corp.	EMC 3075 © Evan-Moor Corp.	EMC 3075 © Evan-Moor Corp.	EMC 3075 © Evan-Moor Corp.
Compare Decimals	Compare Decimals	Compare Decimals	Compare Decimals	Compare Decimals
EMC 3075 © Evan-Moor Corp.	EMC 3075 © Evan-Moor Corp.	EMC 3075 © Evan-Moor Corp.	EMC 3075 © Evan-Moor Corp.	EMC 3075 © Evan-Moor Corp.
Compare Decimals	Compare Decimals	Compare Decimals	Compare Decimals	Compare Decimals
EMC 3075 © Evan-Moor Corp.	EMC 3075 © Evan-Moor Corp.	EMC 3075 © Evan-Moor Corp.	EMC 3075 © Evan-Moor Corp.	EMC 3075 © Evan-Moor Corp.
Compare Decimals	Compare Decimals	Compare Decimals	Compare Decimals	Compare Decimals
EMC 3075 © Evan-Moor Corp.	EMC 3075 © Evan-Moor Corp.	EMC 3075 © Evan-Moor Corp.	EMC 3075 © Evan-Moor Corp.	EMC 3075 © Evan-Moor Corp.
Compare Decimals	Compare Decimals	Compare Decimals	Compare Decimals	Compare Decimals
EMC 3075 © Evan-Moor Corp.	EMC 3075 © Evan-Moor Corp.	EMC 3075 © Evan-Moor Corp.	EMC 3075 © Evan-Moor Corp.	EMC 3075 © Evan-Moor Corp.
Compare Decimals	Compare Decimals	Compare Decimals	Compare Decimals	Compare Decimals
EMC 3075 © Evan-Moor Corp.	EMC 3075 © Evan-Moor Corp.	EMC 3075 © Evan-Moor Corp.	EMC 3075 © Evan-Moor Corp.	EMC 3075 © Evan-Moor Corp.
Compare Decimals	Compare Decimals	Compare Decimals	Compare Decimals	Compare Decimals
EMC 3075 © Evan-Moor Corp.	EMC 3075 © Evan-Moor Corp.	EMC 3075 © Evan-Moor Corp.	EMC 3075 © Evan-Moor Corp.	EMC 3075 © Evan-Moor Corp.
Compare Decimals	Compare Decimals	Compare Decimals	Compare Decimals	Compare Decimals
EMC 3075 © Evan-Moor Corp.	EMC 3075 © Evan-Moor Corp.	EMC 3075 © Evan-Moor Corp.	EMC 3075 © Evan-Moor Corp.	EMC 3075 © Evan-Moor Corp.

Computation Speed Drill

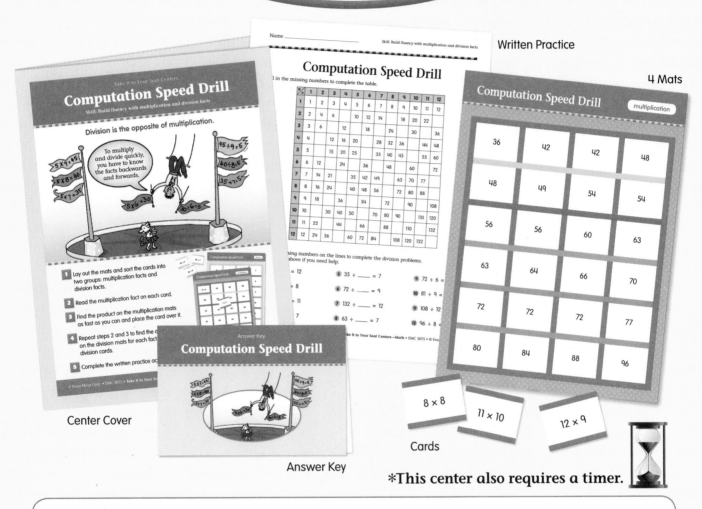

Skill: Build fluency with multiplication and division facts from 6 through 12

Steps to Follow

1. **Prepare the center.** (See page 3.) Make sure that students have access to a timer.

2. **Introduce the center.** State the goal. Say: *You will work as quickly as you can to find the products and quotients on the mats for the multiplication and division facts on the cards.*

3. **Teach the skill.** Demonstrate how to use the center with individual students or small groups.

4. **Practice the skill.** Have students use the center independently or with a partner.

Contents

Computation Speed Drill

Fill in the missing numbers to complete the table.

×/÷	1	2	3	4	5	6	7	8	9	10	11	12
1	1	2	3	4	5	6	7	8	9	10	11	12
2	2	4	6		10	12	14		18	20	22	
3	3	6		12		18		24		30		36
4	4		12	16	20		28	32	36		44	48
5	5		15	20	25		35	40	45		55	60
6	6	12		24		36		48		60		72
7	7	14	21		35	42	49		63	70	77	
8	8	16	24		40	48	56		72	80	88	
9	9	18		36		54		72		90		108
10	10		30	40	50		70	80	90		110	120
11	11	22		44		66		88		110		132
12	12	24	36		60	72	84		108	120	132	

Write the missing numbers on the lines to complete the division problems.
Use the table above if you need help.

1 ____ ÷ 4 = 12

2 ____ ÷ 7 = 8

3 ____ ÷ 10 = 11

4 ____ ÷ 12 = 7

5 35 ÷ ____ = 7

6 72 ÷ ____ = 9

7 132 ÷ ____ = 12

8 63 ÷ ____ = 7

9 72 ÷ 6 = ____

10 81 ÷ 9 = ____

11 108 ÷ 12 = ____

12 96 ÷ 8 = ____

Computation Speed Drill

Skill: Build fluency with multiplication and division facts

Division is the opposite of multiplication.

1. Lay out the mats and sort the cards into two groups: multiplication facts and division facts.

2. Read the multiplication fact on each card.

3. Find the product on the multiplication mats as fast as you can and place the card over it.

4. Repeat steps 2 and 3 to find the quotient on the division mats for each fact on the division cards.

5. Complete the written practice activity.

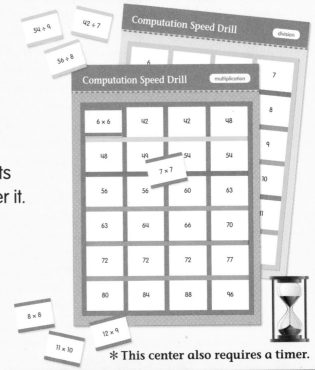

✱ This center also requires a timer.

Written Practice

Computation Speed Drill

Fill in the missing numbers to complete the table.

×÷	1	2	3	4	5	6	7	8	9	10	11	12
1	1	2	3	4	5	6	7	8	9	10	11	12
2	2	4	6	8	10	12	14	16	18	20	22	24
3	3	6	9	12	15	18	21	24	27	30	33	36
4	4	8	12	16	20	24	28	32	36	40	44	48
5	5	10	15	20	25	30	35	40	45	50	55	60
6	6	12	18	24	30	36	42	48	54	60	66	72
7	7	14	21	28	35	42	49	56	63	70	77	84
8	8	16	24	32	40	48	56	64	72	80	88	96
9	9	18	27	36	45	54	63	72	81	90	99	108
10	10	20	30	40	50	60	70	80	90	100	110	120
11	11	22	33	44	55	66	77	88	99	110	121	132
12	12	24	36	48	60	72	84	96	108	120	132	144

Write the missing numbers on the lines to complete the division problems.
Use the table above if you need help.

1. $48 \div 4 = 12$

2. $56 \div 7 = 8$

3. $110 \div 10 = 11$

4. $84 \div 12 = 7$

5. $35 \div 5 = 7$

6. $72 \div 8 = 9$

7. $132 \div 11 = 12$

8. $63 \div 9 = 7$

9. $72 \div 6 = 12$

10. $81 \div 9 = 9$

11. $108 \div 12 = 9$

12. $96 \div 8 = 12$

Answer Key

Computation Speed Drill

Placement of cards with the same products
and cards with inverse equations will vary.

Computation Speed Drill — multiplication

6 × 6	6 × 7	7 × 6	6 × 8
8 × 6	7 × 7	6 × 9	9 × 6
7 × 8	8 × 7	10 × 6	7 × 9
9 × 7	8 × 8	11 × 6	10 × 7
6 × 12	8 × 9	9 × 8	7 × 11
8 × 10	7 × 12	8 × 11	8 × 12

Computation Speed Drill — multiplication

2 × 12	3 × 12	4 × 12	5 × 12
12 × 6	9 × 9	12 × 7	11 × 8
9 × 10	10 × 9	12 × 8	9 × 11
11 × 9	10 × 10	9 × 12	12 × 9
10 × 11	11 × 10	10 × 12	12 × 10
11 × 11	11 × 12	12 × 11	12 × 12

Computation Speed Drill — division

42 ÷ 7	48 ÷ 8	54 ÷ 9	42 ÷ 6
49 ÷ 7	56 ÷ 8	63 ÷ 9	48 ÷ 6
56 ÷ 7	64 ÷ 8	72 ÷ 9	54 ÷ 6
63 ÷ 7	72 ÷ 8	81 ÷ 9	60 ÷ 6
70 ÷ 7	80 ÷ 8	66 ÷ 6	77 ÷ 7
88 ÷ 8	72 ÷ 6	84 ÷ 7	96 ÷ 8

Computation Speed Drill — division

24 ÷ 12	36 ÷ 12	48 ÷ 12	60 ÷ 12
72 ÷ 12	77 ÷ 11	84 ÷ 12	80 ÷ 10
88 ÷ 11	96 ÷ 12	90 ÷ 10	99 ÷ 11
108 ÷ 12	100 ÷ 10	120 ÷ 12	110 ÷ 11
99 ÷ 9	110 ÷ 10	121 ÷ 11	132 ÷ 12
108 ÷ 9	120 ÷ 10	132 ÷ 11	144 ÷ 12

Computation Speed Drill

36	42	42	48
48	49	54	54
56	56	60	63
63	64	66	70
72	72	72	77
80	84	88	96

Computation Speed Drill

24	36	48	60
72	81	84	88
90	90	96	99
99	100	108	108
110	110	120	120
121	132	132	144

Computation Speed Drill

6	6	6	7
7	7	7	8
8	8	8	9
9	9	9	10
10	10	11	11
11	12	12	12

Computation Speed Drill

2	3	4	5
6	7	7	8
8	8	9	9
9	10	10	10
11	11	11	11
12	12	12	12

6 × 6	6 × 7	6 × 8	6 × 9
10 × 6	11 × 6	6 × 12	7 × 6
7 × 7	7 × 8	7 × 9	10 × 7
7 × 11	7 × 12	8 × 6	8 × 7
8 × 8	8 × 9	8 × 10	8 × 11
8 × 12	9 × 6	9 × 7	9 × 8

Computation Speed Drill

EMC 3075

© Evan-Moor Corp.

Computation Speed Drill

EMC 3075

© Evan-Moor Corp.

Computation Speed Drill

EMC 3075

© Evan-Moor Corp.

Computation Speed Drill

EMC 3075

© Evan-Moor Corp.

Computation Speed Drill

EMC 3075

© Evan-Moor Corp.

Computation Speed Drill

EMC 3075

© Evan-Moor Corp.

Computation Speed Drill

EMC 3075

© Evan-Moor Corp.

Computation Speed Drill

EMC 3075

© Evan-Moor Corp.

Computation Speed Drill

EMC 3075

© Evan-Moor Corp.

Computation Speed Drill

EMC 3075

© Evan-Moor Corp.

Computation Speed Drill

EMC 3075

© Evan-Moor Corp.

Computation Speed Drill

EMC 3075

© Evan-Moor Corp.

Computation Speed Drill

EMC 3075

© Evan-Moor Corp.

Computation Speed Drill

EMC 3075

© Evan-Moor Corp.

Computation Speed Drill

EMC 3075

© Evan-Moor Corp.

Computation Speed Drill

EMC 3075

© Evan-Moor Corp.

Computation Speed Drill

EMC 3075

© Evan-Moor Corp.

Computation Speed Drill

EMC 3075

© Evan-Moor Corp.

Computation Speed Drill

EMC 3075

© Evan-Moor Corp.

Computation Speed Drill

EMC 3075

© Evan-Moor Corp.

Computation Speed Drill

EMC 3075

© Evan-Moor Corp.

Computation Speed Drill

EMC 3075

© Evan-Moor Corp.

Computation Speed Drill

EMC 3075

© Evan-Moor Corp.

Computation Speed Drill

EMC 3075

© Evan-Moor Corp.

9×9	9×10	9×11	9×12
10×9	10×10	10×11	10×12
11×8	11×9	11×10	11×11
11×12	2×12	3×12	4×12
5×12	12×6	12×7	12×8
12×9	12×10	12×11	12×12

Computation Speed Drill

EMC 3075

© Evan-Moor Corp.

Computation Speed Drill

EMC 3075

© Evan-Moor Corp.

Computation Speed Drill

EMC 3075

© Evan-Moor Corp.

Computation Speed Drill

EMC 3075

© Evan-Moor Corp.

Computation Speed Drill

EMC 3075

© Evan-Moor Corp.

Computation Speed Drill

EMC 3075

© Evan-Moor Corp.

Computation Speed Drill

EMC 3075

© Evan-Moor Corp.

Computation Speed Drill

EMC 3075

© Evan-Moor Corp.

Computation Speed Drill

EMC 3075

© Evan-Moor Corp.

Computation Speed Drill

EMC 3075

© Evan-Moor Corp.

Computation Speed Drill

EMC 3075

© Evan-Moor Corp.

Computation Speed Drill

EMC 3075

© Evan-Moor Corp.

Computation Speed Drill

EMC 3075

© Evan-Moor Corp.

Computation Speed Drill

EMC 3075

© Evan-Moor Corp.

Computation Speed Drill

EMC 3075

© Evan-Moor Corp.

Computation Speed Drill

EMC 3075

© Evan-Moor Corp.

Computation Speed Drill

EMC 3075

© Evan-Moor Corp.

Computation Speed Drill

EMC 3075

© Evan-Moor Corp.

Computation Speed Drill

EMC 3075

© Evan-Moor Corp.

Computation Speed Drill

EMC 3075

© Evan-Moor Corp.

Computation Speed Drill

EMC 3075

© Evan-Moor Corp.

Computation Speed Drill

EMC 3075

© Evan-Moor Corp.

Computation Speed Drill

EMC 3075

© Evan-Moor Corp.

Computation Speed Drill

EMC 3075

© Evan-Moor Corp.

$42 \div 6$	$48 \div 6$	$54 \div 6$	$60 \div 6$
$66 \div 6$	$72 \div 6$	$42 \div 7$	$49 \div 7$
$56 \div 7$	$63 \div 7$	$70 \div 7$	$77 \div 7$
$84 \div 7$	$48 \div 8$	$56 \div 8$	$64 \div 8$
$72 \div 8$	$80 \div 8$	$88 \div 8$	$96 \div 8$
$54 \div 9$	$63 \div 9$	$72 \div 9$	$81 \div 9$

Computation Speed Drill	Computation Speed Drill	Computation Speed Drill	Computation Speed Drill
EMC 3075	EMC 3075	EMC 3075	EMC 3075
© Evan-Moor Corp.	© Evan-Moor Corp.	© Evan-Moor Corp.	© Evan-Moor Corp.
Computation Speed Drill	Computation Speed Drill	Computation Speed Drill	Computation Speed Drill
EMC 3075	EMC 3075	EMC 3075	EMC 3075
© Evan-Moor Corp.	© Evan-Moor Corp.	© Evan-Moor Corp.	© Evan-Moor Corp.
Computation Speed Drill	Computation Speed Drill	Computation Speed Drill	Computation Speed Drill
EMC 3075	EMC 3075	EMC 3075	EMC 3075
© Evan-Moor Corp.	© Evan-Moor Corp.	© Evan-Moor Corp.	© Evan-Moor Corp.
Computation Speed Drill	Computation Speed Drill	Computation Speed Drill	Computation Speed Drill
EMC 3075	EMC 3075	EMC 3075	EMC 3075
© Evan-Moor Corp.	© Evan-Moor Corp.	© Evan-Moor Corp.	© Evan-Moor Corp.
Computation Speed Drill	Computation Speed Drill	Computation Speed Drill	Computation Speed Drill
EMC 3075	EMC 3075	EMC 3075	EMC 3075
© Evan-Moor Corp.	© Evan-Moor Corp.	© Evan-Moor Corp.	© Evan-Moor Corp.
Computation Speed Drill	Computation Speed Drill	Computation Speed Drill	Computation Speed Drill
EMC 3075	EMC 3075	EMC 3075	EMC 3075
© Evan-Moor Corp.	© Evan-Moor Corp.	© Evan-Moor Corp.	© Evan-Moor Corp.

99 ÷ 9	108 ÷ 9	80 ÷ 10	90 ÷ 10
100 ÷ 10	110 ÷ 10	120 ÷ 10	77 ÷ 11
88 ÷ 11	99 ÷ 11	110 ÷ 11	121 ÷ 11
132 ÷ 11	24 ÷ 12	36 ÷ 12	48 ÷ 12
60 ÷ 12	72 ÷ 12	84 ÷ 12	96 ÷ 12
108 ÷ 12	120 ÷ 12	132 ÷ 12	144 ÷ 12

Computation Speed Drill

EMC 3075

© Evan-Moor Corp.

Computation Speed Drill

EMC 3075

© Evan-Moor Corp.

Computation Speed Drill

EMC 3075

© Evan-Moor Corp.

Computation Speed Drill

EMC 3075

© Evan-Moor Corp.

Computation Speed Drill

EMC 3075

© Evan-Moor Corp.

Computation Speed Drill

EMC 3075

© Evan-Moor Corp.

Computation Speed Drill

EMC 3075

© Evan-Moor Corp.

Computation Speed Drill

EMC 3075

© Evan-Moor Corp.

Computation Speed Drill

EMC 3075

© Evan-Moor Corp.

Computation Speed Drill

EMC 3075

© Evan-Moor Corp.

Computation Speed Drill

EMC 3075

© Evan-Moor Corp.

Computation Speed Drill

EMC 3075

© Evan-Moor Corp.

Computation Speed Drill

EMC 3075

© Evan-Moor Corp.

Computation Speed Drill

EMC 3075

© Evan-Moor Corp.

Computation Speed Drill

EMC 3075

© Evan-Moor Corp.

Computation Speed Drill

EMC 3075

© Evan-Moor Corp.

Computation Speed Drill

EMC 3075

© Evan-Moor Corp.

Computation Speed Drill

EMC 3075

© Evan-Moor Corp.

Computation Speed Drill

EMC 3075

© Evan-Moor Corp.

Computation Speed Drill

EMC 3075

© Evan-Moor Corp.

Computation Speed Drill

EMC 3075

© Evan-Moor Corp.

Computation Speed Drill

EMC 3075

© Evan-Moor Corp.

Computation Speed Drill

EMC 3075

© Evan-Moor Corp.

Computation Speed Drill

EMC 3075

© Evan-Moor Corp.

Add and Subtract Fractions

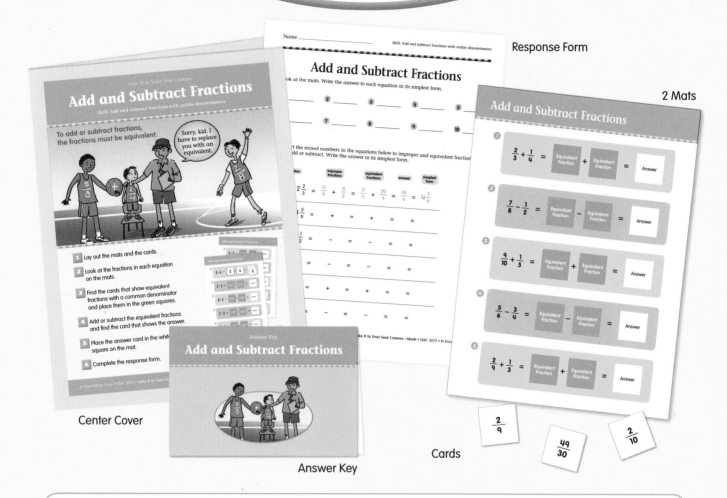

Response Form

2 Mats

Center Cover

Answer Key

Cards

Skill: Add and subtract fractions with unlike denominators

Steps to Follow

1. **Prepare the center.** (See page 3.)

2. **Introduce the center.** State the goal. Say: *You will add and subtract fractions with different denominators by finding equivalent fractions with a common denominator.*

3. **Teach the skill.** Demonstrate how to use the center with individual students or small groups.

4. **Practice the skill.** Have students use the center independently or with a partner.

Contents

Add and Subtract Fractions

Look at the mats. Write the answer to each equation in its simplest form.

1 _____   2 _____   3 _____   4 _____   5 _____

6 _____   7 _____   8 _____   9 _____   10 _____

Convert the mixed numbers in the equations below to improper and equivalent fractions. Then add or subtract. Write the answer in its simplest form.

equation	improper fractions	equivalent fractions	answer	simplest form
$1\frac{8}{9} + 2\frac{2}{3} =$	$\frac{17}{9} + \frac{8}{3} =$	$\frac{17}{9} + \frac{24}{9} =$	$\frac{41}{9} =$	$4\frac{5}{9}$
$3\frac{3}{4} + 4\frac{3}{8} =$	$+$ $=$	$+$ $=$	$=$	
$4\frac{2}{3} - 1\frac{1}{2} =$	$-$ $=$	$-$ $=$	$=$	
$3\frac{3}{4} - 2\frac{2}{3} =$	$-$ $=$	$-$ $=$	$=$	
$2\frac{5}{6} + 7\frac{1}{4} =$	$+$ $=$	$+$ $=$	$=$	
$10\frac{7}{8} - 5\frac{3}{4} =$	$-$ $=$	$-$ $=$	$=$	

Add and Subtract Fractions

Skill: Add and subtract fractions with unlike denominators

To add or subtract fractions, the fractions must be equivalent.

Sorry, kid. I have to replace you with an equivalent.

1 Lay out the mats and the cards.

2 Look at the fractions in each equation on the mats.

3 Find the cards that show equivalent fractions with a common denominator and place them in the green squares.

4 Add or subtract the equivalent fractions and find the card that shows the answer.

5 Place the answer card in the white square on the mat.

6 Complete the response form.

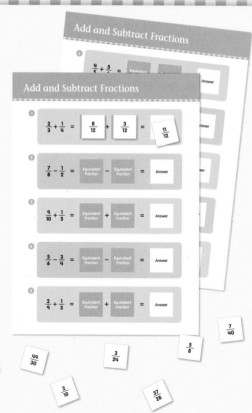

Add and Subtract Fractions

Answer Key

(fold)

Response Form

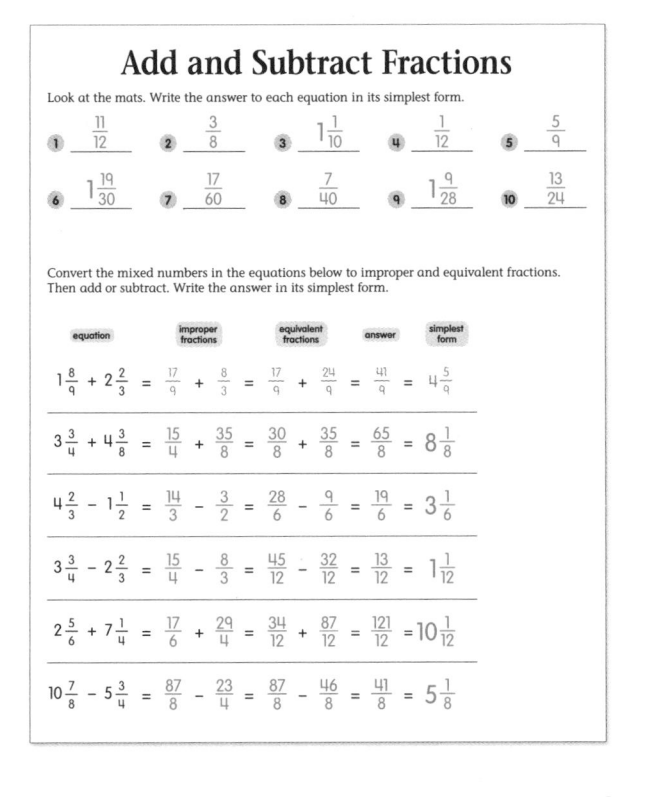

Add and Subtract Fractions

Look at the mats. Write the answer to each equation in its simplest form.

1. $\dfrac{11}{12}$ 2. $\dfrac{3}{8}$ 3. $1\dfrac{1}{10}$ 4. $\dfrac{1}{12}$ 5. $\dfrac{5}{9}$

6. $1\dfrac{19}{30}$ 7. $\dfrac{17}{60}$ 8. $\dfrac{7}{40}$ 9. $1\dfrac{9}{28}$ 10. $\dfrac{13}{24}$

Convert the mixed numbers in the equations below to improper and equivalent fractions. Then add or subtract. Write the answer in its simplest form.

equation	improper fractions	equivalent fractions	answer	simplest form
$1\dfrac{8}{9} + 2\dfrac{2}{3} =$	$\dfrac{17}{9} + \dfrac{8}{3} =$	$\dfrac{17}{9} + \dfrac{24}{9} =$	$\dfrac{41}{9} =$	$4\dfrac{5}{9}$
$3\dfrac{3}{4} + 4\dfrac{3}{8} =$	$\dfrac{15}{4} + \dfrac{35}{8} =$	$\dfrac{30}{8} + \dfrac{35}{8} =$	$\dfrac{65}{8} =$	$8\dfrac{1}{8}$
$4\dfrac{2}{3} - 1\dfrac{1}{2} =$	$\dfrac{14}{3} - \dfrac{3}{2} =$	$\dfrac{28}{6} - \dfrac{9}{6} =$	$\dfrac{19}{6} =$	$3\dfrac{1}{6}$
$3\dfrac{3}{4} - 2\dfrac{2}{3} =$	$\dfrac{15}{4} - \dfrac{8}{3} =$	$\dfrac{45}{12} - \dfrac{32}{12} =$	$\dfrac{13}{12} =$	$1\dfrac{1}{12}$
$2\dfrac{5}{6} + 7\dfrac{1}{4} =$	$\dfrac{17}{6} + \dfrac{29}{4} =$	$\dfrac{34}{12} + \dfrac{87}{12} =$	$\dfrac{121}{12} =$	$10\dfrac{1}{12}$
$10\dfrac{7}{8} - 5\dfrac{3}{4} =$	$\dfrac{87}{8} - \dfrac{23}{4} =$	$\dfrac{87}{8} - \dfrac{46}{8} =$	$\dfrac{41}{8} =$	$5\dfrac{1}{8}$

Add and Subtract Fractions

Add and Subtract Fractions

1. $\dfrac{2}{3} + \dfrac{1}{4} = \boxed{\dfrac{8}{12}} + \boxed{\dfrac{3}{12}} = \boxed{\dfrac{11}{12}}$

2. $\dfrac{7}{8} - \dfrac{1}{2} = \boxed{\dfrac{7}{8}} - \boxed{\dfrac{4}{8}} = \boxed{\dfrac{3}{8}}$

3. $\dfrac{9}{10} + \dfrac{1}{5} = \boxed{\dfrac{9}{10}} + \boxed{\dfrac{2}{10}} = \boxed{\dfrac{11}{10}}$

4. $\dfrac{5}{6} - \dfrac{3}{4} = \boxed{\dfrac{10}{12}} - \boxed{\dfrac{9}{12}} = \boxed{\dfrac{1}{12}}$

5. $\dfrac{2}{9} + \dfrac{1}{3} = \boxed{\dfrac{2}{9}} + \boxed{\dfrac{3}{9}} = \boxed{\dfrac{5}{9}}$

Add and Subtract Fractions

6. $\dfrac{4}{5} + \dfrac{5}{6} = \boxed{\dfrac{24}{30}} + \boxed{\dfrac{25}{30}} = \boxed{\dfrac{49}{30}}$

7. $\dfrac{7}{10} - \dfrac{5}{12} = \boxed{\dfrac{42}{60}} - \boxed{\dfrac{25}{60}} = \boxed{\dfrac{17}{60}}$

8. $\dfrac{4}{5} - \dfrac{5}{8} = \boxed{\dfrac{32}{40}} - \boxed{\dfrac{25}{40}} = \boxed{\dfrac{7}{40}}$

9. $\dfrac{3}{4} + \dfrac{4}{7} = \boxed{\dfrac{21}{28}} + \boxed{\dfrac{16}{28}} = \boxed{\dfrac{37}{28}}$

10. $\dfrac{2}{3} - \dfrac{1}{8} = \boxed{\dfrac{16}{24}} - \boxed{\dfrac{3}{24}} = \boxed{\dfrac{13}{24}}$

Add and Subtract Fractions

1 $\dfrac{2}{3} + \dfrac{1}{4}$ =   Equivalent Fraction   **+**   Equivalent Fraction   **=**   Answer

2 $\dfrac{7}{8} - \dfrac{1}{2}$ =   Equivalent Fraction   **−**   Equivalent Fraction   **=**   Answer

3 $\dfrac{9}{10} + \dfrac{1}{5}$ =   Equivalent Fraction   **+**   Equivalent Fraction   **=**   Answer

4 $\dfrac{5}{6} - \dfrac{3}{4}$ =   Equivalent Fraction   **−**   Equivalent Fraction   **=**   Answer

5 $\dfrac{2}{9} + \dfrac{1}{3}$ =   Equivalent Fraction   **+**   Equivalent Fraction   **=**   Answer

Add and Subtract Fractions

6

$$\frac{4}{5} + \frac{5}{6} =$$ | Equivalent Fraction | **+** | Equivalent Fraction | **=** | Answer

7

$$\frac{7}{10} - \frac{5}{12} =$$ | Equivalent Fraction | **−** | Equivalent Fraction | **=** | Answer

8

$$\frac{4}{5} - \frac{5}{8} =$$ | Equivalent Fraction | **−** | Equivalent Fraction | **=** | Answer

9

$$\frac{3}{4} + \frac{4}{7} =$$ | Equivalent Fraction | **+** | Equivalent Fraction | **=** | Answer

10

$$\frac{2}{3} - \frac{1}{8} =$$ | Equivalent Fraction | **−** | Equivalent Fraction | **=** | Answer

$\dfrac{11}{10}$	$\dfrac{3}{12}$	$\dfrac{8}{12}$	$\dfrac{1}{12}$	$\dfrac{9}{12}$	$\dfrac{5}{8}$
$\dfrac{9}{10}$	$\dfrac{2}{10}$	$\dfrac{10}{12}$	$\dfrac{7}{8}$	$\dfrac{4}{8}$	$\dfrac{3}{8}$
$\dfrac{32}{40}$	$\dfrac{21}{28}$	$\dfrac{2}{9}$	$\dfrac{3}{9}$	$\dfrac{5}{9}$	$\dfrac{4}{12}$
$\dfrac{25}{40}$	$\dfrac{16}{28}$	$\dfrac{24}{30}$	$\dfrac{42}{60}$	$\dfrac{16}{24}$	$\dfrac{3}{24}$
$\dfrac{7}{40}$	$\dfrac{37}{28}$	$\dfrac{25}{30}$	$\dfrac{25}{60}$	$\dfrac{13}{24}$	$\dfrac{2}{3}$
$\dfrac{5}{12}$	$\dfrac{11}{12}$	$\dfrac{49}{30}$	$\dfrac{17}{60}$	$\dfrac{38}{30}$	$\dfrac{5}{8}$

Add and Subtract Fractions	Add and Subtract Fractions	Add and Subtract Fractions	Add and Subtract Fractions	Add and Subtract Fractions	Add and Subtract Fractions
EMC 3075 © Evan-Moor Corp.	**EMC 3075** © Evan-Moor Corp.	**EMC 3075** © Evan-Moor Corp.	**EMC 3075** © Evan-Moor Corp.	**EMC 3075** © Evan-Moor Corp.	**EMC 3075** © Evan-Moor Corp.
Add and Subtract Fractions	Add and Subtract Fractions	Add and Subtract Fractions	Add and Subtract Fractions	Add and Subtract Fractions	Add and Subtract Fractions
EMC 3075 © Evan-Moor Corp.	**EMC 3075** © Evan-Moor Corp.	**EMC 3075** © Evan-Moor Corp.	**EMC 3075** © Evan-Moor Corp.	**EMC 3075** © Evan-Moor Corp.	**EMC 3075** © Evan-Moor Corp.
Add and Subtract Fractions	Add and Subtract Fractions	Add and Subtract Fractions	Add and Subtract Fractions	Add and Subtract Fractions	Add and Subtract Fractions
EMC 3075 © Evan-Moor Corp.	**EMC 3075** © Evan-Moor Corp.	**EMC 3075** © Evan-Moor Corp.	**EMC 3075** © Evan-Moor Corp.	**EMC 3075** © Evan-Moor Corp.	**EMC 3075** © Evan-Moor Corp.
Add and Subtract Fractions	Add and Subtract Fractions	Add and Subtract Fractions	Add and Subtract Fractions	Add and Subtract Fractions	Add and Subtract Fractions
EMC 3075 © Evan-Moor Corp.	**EMC 3075** © Evan-Moor Corp.	**EMC 3075** © Evan-Moor Corp.	**EMC 3075** © Evan-Moor Corp.	**EMC 3075** © Evan-Moor Corp.	**EMC 3075** © Evan-Moor Corp.
Add and Subtract Fractions	Add and Subtract Fractions	Add and Subtract Fractions	Add and Subtract Fractions	Add and Subtract Fractions	Add and Subtract Fractions
EMC 3075 © Evan-Moor Corp.	**EMC 3075** © Evan-Moor Corp.	**EMC 3075** © Evan-Moor Corp.	**EMC 3075** © Evan-Moor Corp.	**EMC 3075** © Evan-Moor Corp.	**EMC 3075** © Evan-Moor Corp.
Add and Subtract Fractions	Add and Subtract Fractions	Add and Subtract Fractions	Add and Subtract Fractions	Add and Subtract Fractions	Add and Subtract Fractions
EMC 3075 © Evan-Moor Corp.	**EMC 3075** © Evan-Moor Corp.	**EMC 3075** © Evan-Moor Corp.	**EMC 3075** © Evan-Moor Corp.	**EMC 3075** © Evan-Moor Corp.	**EMC 3075** © Evan-Moor Corp.

Real-World Word Problems

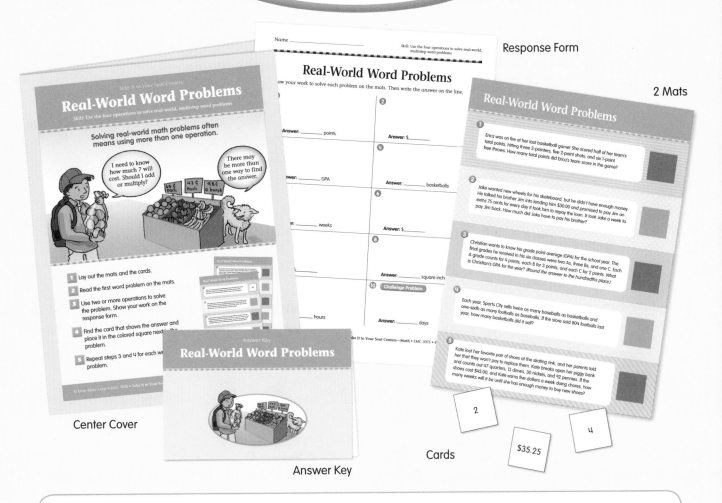

Center Cover

Answer Key

Cards

Response Form

2 Mats

Skill: Use the four operations to solve real-world, multistep word problems

Steps to Follow

1. **Prepare the center.** (See page 3.)

2. **Introduce the center.** State the goal. Say: *You will read and solve word problems that require two or more operations.*

3. **Teach the skill.** Demonstrate how to use the center with individual students or small groups.

4. **Practice the skill.** Have students use the center independently or with a partner.

Contents

Name ______________________

Skill: Use the four operations to solve real-world, multistep word problems

Real-World Word Problems

Show your work to solve each problem on the mats. Then write the answer on the line.

1

Answer: ________ points

2

Answer: $________

3

Answer: ________ GPA

4

Answer: ________ basketballs

5

Answer: ________ weeks

6

Answer: $________

7

Answer: $________

8

Answer: ________ square inches

9

Answer: ________ hours

10 Challenge Problem

Answer: ________ days

Real-World Word Problems

Skill: Use the four operations to solve real-world, multistep word problems

Solving real-world math problems often means using more than one operation.

1. Lay out the mats and the cards.

2. Read the first word problem on the mats.

3. Use two or more operations to solve the problem. Show your work on the response form.

4. Find the card that shows the answer and place it in the colored square next to the problem.

5. Repeat steps 3 and 4 for each word problem.

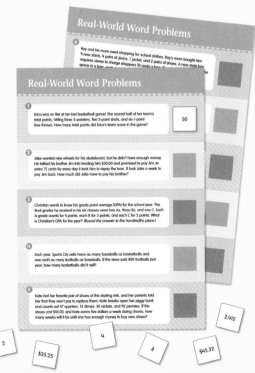

Real-World Word Problems

Show your work to solve each problem on the mats. Then write the answer on the line.

1
Answer: 50 points

2
Answer: $35.25

3
Answer: 3.17 GPA

4
Answer: 2,412 basketballs

5
Answer: 6 weeks

6
Answer: $0.50

7
Answer: $44.97

8
Answer: 384 square inches

9
Answer: $3\frac{1}{2}$ hours

10 Challenge Problem
Answer: 11 days

Response Form

(fold)

Answer Key

Real-World Word Problems

Real-World Word Problems

1. Erica was on fire at her last basketball game! She scored half of her team's total points, hitting three 3-pointers, five 2-point shots, and six 1-point free throws. How many total points did Erica's team score in the game?

50

2. Jake wanted new wheels for his skateboard, but he didn't have enough money. He talked his brother Jim into lending him $30.00 and promised to pay Jim an extra 75 cents for every day it took him to repay the loan. If it took Jake a week to pay Jim back. How much did Jake have to pay his brother?

$35.25

3. Christian wants to know his grade point average (GPA) for the school year. The final grades he received in his six classes were two As, three Bs, and one C. Each A grade counts for 4 points, each B for 3 points, and each C for 2 points. What is Christian's GPA for the year? (Round the answer to the hundredths place.)

3.17

4. Each year, Sports City sells twice as many baseballs as basketballs and one-sixth as many footballs as baseballs. If the store sold 804 footballs last year, how many basketballs did it sell?

2,412

5. Kate lost her favorite pair of shoes at the skating rink, and her parents told her that they won't pay to replace them. Kate breaks open her piggy bank and counts out 47 quarters, 13 dimes, 30 nickels, and 92 pennies. If the shoes cost $45.00, and Kate earns five dollars a week doing chores, how many weeks will it be until she has enough money to buy new shoes?

6

Real-World Word Problems

6. Ray and his mom went shopping for school clothes. Ray's mom bought him 9 new shirts, 1 pairs of jeans, 1 jacket, and 2 pairs of shoes. A new state law requires stores to charge shoppers 10 cents a bag. If each shirt took up $\frac{1}{6}$ of the space in a bag, each pair of jeans took up $\frac{1}{3}$, the jacket took up $\frac{1}{2}$, and pair of shoes $\frac{1}{12}$, how much did Ray's mom have to pay for bags?

$0.50

7. Allison is selling her bike for $85.00, but she had to buy new tires for it first. The tires cost $14.88 each. The bike shop charged $5.25 to put on both tires but gave Allison a $3.50 recycling credit for the old ones. If Allison gets $\frac{1}{10}$ of her asking price, how much money will she clear after deducting the final cost of the tires?

$44.97

8. Tim is making a scale model of the doghouse he wants to build. The model will be $\frac{1}{3}$ the size of the real doghouse. If the base of the real doghouse measures 6 feet long and 4 feet wide, how many square inches will the area be for the base of the scale model?

384

9. Brandon is planning his Sunday. He estimates that cleaning his room will take $\frac{1}{4}$ of the day, his bike ride will take $\frac{1}{8}$, each meal (breakfast, lunch, and dinner will take $\frac{1}{10}$, and his homework will take $\frac{1}{5}$. If he gets up at 8:00 a.m. and goes to bed at 10:00 p.m., about how many hours will he have left to play video games?

$3\frac{1}{2}$

10. Challenge Problem

Andy rides his bike to school. The ride is 2 miles by sidewalk or $2\frac{1}{2}$ miles if he takes the dirt path through the field. On the sidewalk, Andy loses $\frac{1}{8}$ of the air in his tires every 6 miles. On the dirt path, he loses $\frac{1}{10}$ every 5 miles. If Andy rides his bike only to and from school and takes the dirt path on Mondays and Fridays and the sidewalk the other three days, after how many days will his tires be flat?

11

Real-World Word Problems

1 Erica was on fire at her last basketball game! She scored half of her team's total points, hitting three 3-pointers, five 2-point shots, and six 1-point free throws. How many total points did Erica's team score in the game?

2 Jake wanted new wheels for his skateboard, but he didn't have enough money. He talked his brother Jim into lending him $30.00 and promised to pay Jim an extra 75 cents for every day it took him to repay the loan. It took Jake a week to pay Jim back. How much did Jake have to pay his brother?

3 Christian wants to know his grade point average (GPA) for the school year. The final grades he received in his six classes were two As, three Bs, and one C. Each A grade counts for 4 points, each B for 3 points, and each C for 2 points. What is Christian's GPA for the year? *(Round the answer to the hundredths place.)*

4 Each year, Sports City sells twice as many baseballs as basketballs and one-sixth as many footballs as baseballs. If the store sold 804 footballs last year, how many basketballs did it sell?

5 Kate lost her favorite pair of shoes at the skating rink, and her parents told her that they won't pay to replace them. Kate breaks open her piggy bank and counts out 47 quarters, 13 dimes, 30 nickels, and 92 pennies. If the shoes cost $45.00, and Kate earns five dollars a week doing chores, how many weeks will it be until she has enough money to buy new shoes?

Real-World Word Problems

6

Ray and his mom went shopping for school clothes. Ray's mom bought him 9 new shirts, 4 pairs of jeans, 1 jacket, and 2 pairs of shoes. A new state law requires stores to charge shoppers 10 cents a bag. If each shirt took up $\frac{1}{6}$ of the space in a bag, each pair of jeans took up $\frac{1}{3}$, the jacket took up $\frac{2}{3}$, and each pair of shoes $\frac{3}{4}$, how much did Ray's mom have to pay for bags?

7

Allison is selling her bike for $85.00, but she had to buy new tires for it first. The tires cost $14.89 each. The bike shop charged $5.25 to put on both tires but gave Allison a $3.50 recycling credit for the old ones. If Allison gets $\frac{9}{10}$ of her asking price, how much money will she clear after deducting the final cost of the tires?

8

Tim is making a scale model of the doghouse he wants to build. The model will be $\frac{1}{3}$ the size of the real doghouse. If the base of the real doghouse measures 6 feet long and 4 feet wide, how many square inches will the area be for the base of the scale model?

9

Brandon is planning his Sunday. He estimates that cleaning his room will take $\frac{1}{8}$ of the day, his bike ride will take $\frac{1}{8}$, each meal (breakfast, lunch, and dinner) will take $\frac{1}{10}$, and his homework will take $\frac{1}{5}$. If he gets up at 8:00 a.m. and goes to bed at 10:00 p.m., about how many hours will he have left to play video games?

10 Challenge Problem

Andy rides his bike to school. The ride is 2 miles by sidewalk or $2\frac{1}{2}$ miles if he takes the dirt path through the field. On the sidewalk, Andy loses $\frac{1}{8}$ of the air in his tires every 6 miles. On the dirt path, he loses $\frac{1}{10}$ every 5 miles. If Andy rides his bike only to and from school and takes the dirt path on Mondays and Fridays and the sidewalk the other three days, after how many days will his tires be flat?

2	3	3.17	3.16	3.20
$3\frac{1}{2}$	4	<u>6</u>	<u>9</u>	10
11	12	25	50	75
80	268	384	1,152	2,120
2,412	$0.40	$0.50	$0.60	$35.25
$35.75	$37.50	$44.97	$45.22	$46.47

Real-World Word Problems	Real-World Word Problems	Real-World Word Problems	Real-World Word Problems	Real-World Word Problems
EMC 3075 © Evan-Moor Corp.	**EMC 3075** © Evan-Moor Corp.	**EMC 3075** © Evan-Moor Corp.	**EMC 3075** © Evan-Moor Corp.	**EMC 3075** © Evan-Moor Corp.
Real-World Word Problems	Real-World Word Problems	Real-World Word Problems	Real-World Word Problems	Real-World Word Problems
EMC 3075 © Evan-Moor Corp.	**EMC 3075** © Evan-Moor Corp.	**EMC 3075** © Evan-Moor Corp.	**EMC 3075** © Evan-Moor Corp.	**EMC 3075** © Evan-Moor Corp.
Real-World Word Problems	Real-World Word Problems	Real-World Word Problems	Real-World Word Problems	Real-World Word Problems
EMC 3075 © Evan-Moor Corp.	**EMC 3075** © Evan-Moor Corp.	**EMC 3075** © Evan-Moor Corp.	**EMC 3075** © Evan-Moor Corp.	**EMC 3075** © Evan-Moor Corp.
Real-World Word Problems	Real-World Word Problems	Real-World Word Problems	Real-World Word Problems	Real-World Word Problems
EMC 3075 © Evan-Moor Corp.	**EMC 3075** © Evan-Moor Corp.	**EMC 3075** © Evan-Moor Corp.	**EMC 3075** © Evan-Moor Corp.	**EMC 3075** © Evan-Moor Corp.
Real-World Word Problems	Real-World Word Problems	Real-World Word Problems	Real-World Word Problems	Real-World Word Problems
EMC 3075 © Evan-Moor Corp.	**EMC 3075** © Evan-Moor Corp.	**EMC 3075** © Evan-Moor Corp.	**EMC 3075** © Evan-Moor Corp.	**EMC 3075** © Evan-Moor Corp.
Real-World Word Problems	Real-World Word Problems	Real-World Word Problems	Real-World Word Problems	Real-World Word Problems
EMC 3075 © Evan-Moor Corp.	**EMC 3075** © Evan-Moor Corp.	**EMC 3075** © Evan-Moor Corp.	**EMC 3075** © Evan-Moor Corp.	**EMC 3075** © Evan-Moor Corp.

Equivalent Measurements

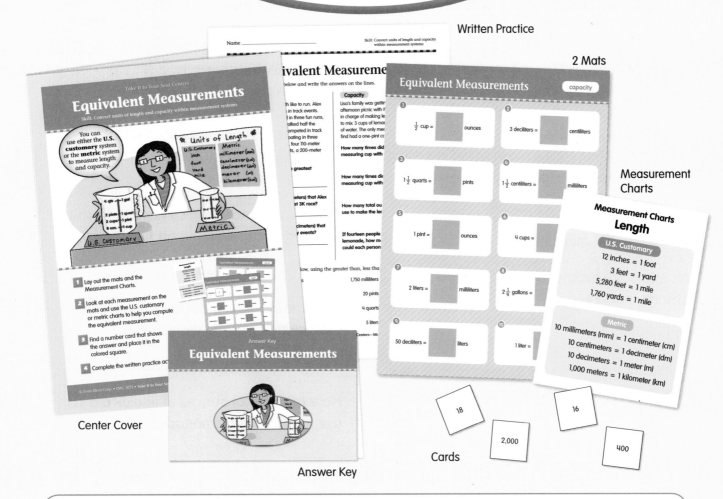

Written Practice

2 Mats

Measurement Charts

Center Cover

Answer Key

Cards

Skill: Convert units of length and capacity within measurement systems (U.S. customary and metric)

Steps to Follow

1. **Prepare the center.** (See page 3.)

2. **Introduce the center.** State the goal. Say: *You will compute equivalent measurements of length and capacity within the U.S. customary and metric systems.*

3. **Teach the skill.** Demonstrate how to use the center with individual students or small groups.

4. **Practice the skill.** Have students use the center independently or with a partner.

Contents

Equivalent Measurements

Solve the word problems below and write the answers on the lines.

Length

Alex and his brother Max both like to run. Alex likes fun runs. Max competes in track events. During May, Alex participated in three fun runs, a 2.5K and two 3Ks, but he walked half the distance in each event. Max competed in track events every weekend, participating in three 800-meter long-distance runs, four 110-meter hurdles, three 200-meter sprints, a 200-meter relay, and a 400-meter relay.

In total, which brother ran the greatest distance during May?

_____

What is the total distance (in meters) that Alex ran in the 2.5K race and the first 3K race?

_____

What is the total distance (in decimeters) that Max ran in the hurdles and relay events?

_____

Capacity

Lisa's family was getting ready for a Sunday afternoon picnic with the neighbors. Lisa was in charge of making lemonade. She needed to mix 3 cups of lemon juice with 2 gallons of water. The only measuring cup Lisa could find had a one-pint capacity.

How many times did Lisa have to fill the measuring cup with lemon juice?

_____

How many times did Lisa have to fill the measuring cup with water?

_____

How many total ounces of liquids did Lisa use to make the lemonade?

_____

If fourteen people at the picnic wanted lemonade, how many 10-ounce glasses could each person have?

_____

Compare the measurements below, using the greater than, less than, and equal to symbols.

7 yards $<$ 300 inches

100,000 cm $\bigcirc$ 1 km

15,000 mm $\bigcirc$ 15 dm

15,000 inches $\bigcirc$ $\frac{1}{4}$ mile

1,750 milliliters $\bigcirc$ $1\frac{1}{2}$ liters

20 pints $\bigcirc$ 2 gallons

4 quarts $\bigcirc$ 128 ounces

5 liters $\bigcirc$ 600 centiliters

Equivalent Measurements

Skill: Convert units of length and capacity within measurement systems

> You can use either the **U.S. customary** system or the **metric** system to measure length and capacity.

1. Lay out the mats and the Measurement Charts.

2. Look at each measurement on the mats and use the U.S. customary or metric charts to help you compute the equivalent measurement.

3. Find a number card that shows the answer and place it in the colored square.

4. Complete the written practice activity.

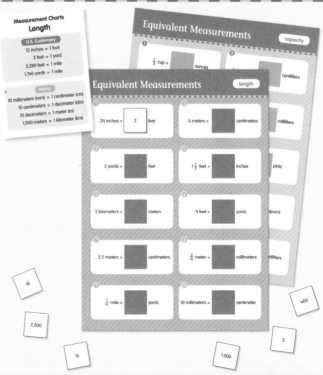

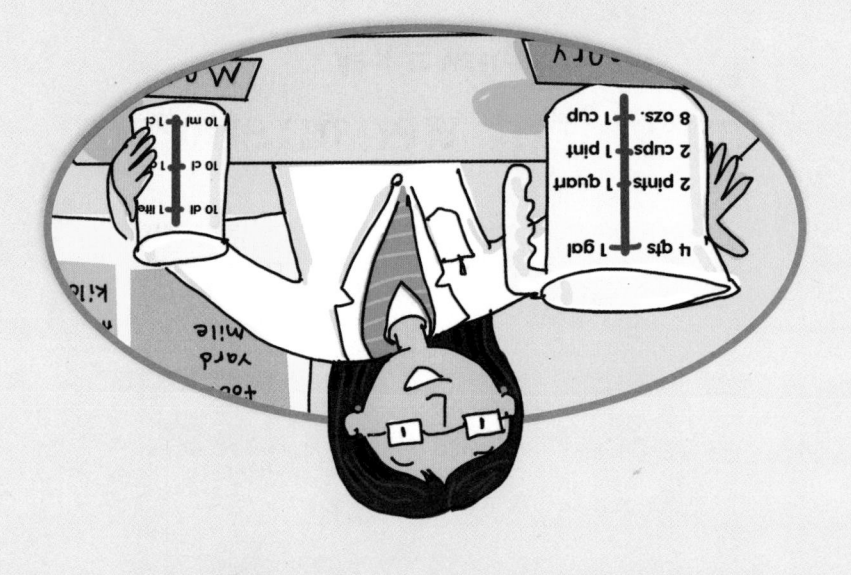

Equivalent Measurements

Answer Key

(fold)

Written Practice

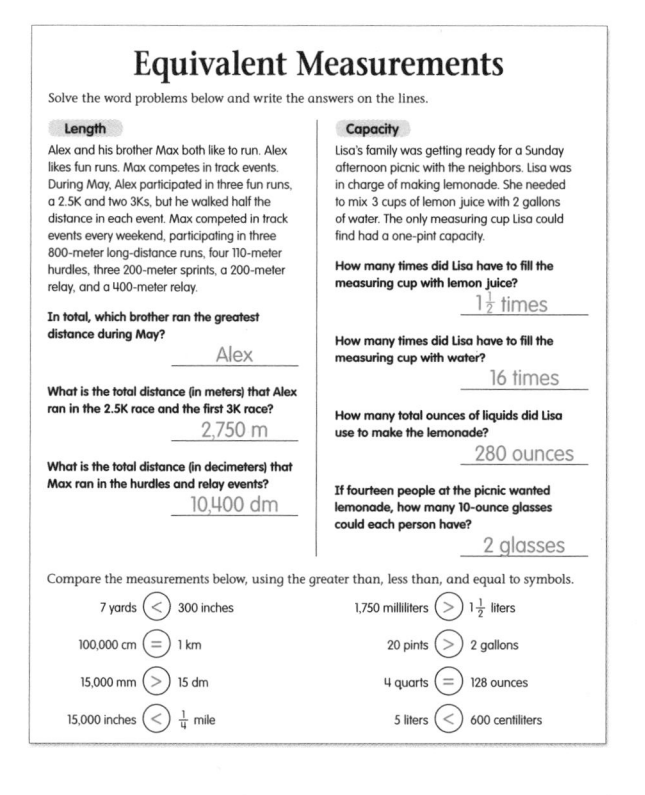

Equivalent Measurements

Solve the word problems below and write the answers on the lines.

Length

Alex and his brother Max both like to run. Alex likes fun runs. Max competes in track events. During May, Alex participated in three fun runs, a 2.5K and two 3Ks, but he walked half the distance in each event. Max competed in track events every weekend, participating in three 800-meter long-distance runs, four 110-meter hurdles, three 200-meter sprints, a 200-meter relay, and a 400-meter relay.

In total, which brother ran the greatest distance during May?

Alex

What is the total distance (in meters) that Alex ran in the 2.5K race and the first 3K race?

2,750 m

What is the total distance (in decimeters) that Max ran in the hurdles and relay events?

10,400 dm

Capacity

Lisa's family was getting ready for a Sunday afternoon picnic with the neighbors. Lisa was in charge of making lemonade. She needed to mix 3 cups of lemon juice with 2 gallons of water. The only measuring cup Lisa could find had a one-pint capacity.

How many times did Lisa have to fill the measuring cup with lemon juice?

$1\frac{1}{2}$ times

How many times did Lisa have to fill the measuring cup with water?

16 times

How many total ounces of liquids did Lisa use to make the lemonade?

280 ounces

If fourteen people at the picnic wanted lemonade, how many 10-ounce glasses could each person have?

2 glasses

Compare the measurements below, using the greater than, less than, and equal to symbols.

7 yards $<$ 300 inches

100,000 cm $=$ 1 km

15,000 mm $>$ 15 dm

15,000 inches $<$ $\frac{1}{4}$ mile

1,750 milliliters $>$ $1\frac{1}{2}$ liters

20 pints $>$ 2 gallons

4 quarts $=$ 128 ounces

5 liters $<$ 600 centiliters

Equivalent Measurements

Equivalent Measurements — length

1	24 inches = **2** feet
2	4 meters = **400** centimeters
3	5 yards = **15** feet
4	$1\frac{1}{2}$ feet = **18** inches
5	2 kilometers = **2,000** meters
6	9 feet = **3** yards
7	2.5 meters = **250** centimeters
8	$\frac{3}{4}$ meter = **750** millimeters
9	$\frac{1}{4}$ mile = **440** yards
10	10 millimeters = **1** centimeter

Equivalent Measurements — capacity

1	$\frac{1}{2}$ cup = **4** ounces
2	3 deciliters = **30** centiliters
3	$1\frac{1}{2}$ quarts = **3** pints
4	$1\frac{1}{2}$ centiliters = **15** milliliters
5	1 pint = **16** ounces
6	4 cups = **2** pints
7	2 liters = **2,000** milliliters
8	$2\frac{1}{4}$ gallons = **9** quarts
9	50 deciliters = **5** liters
10	1 liter = **100** centiliters

Equivalent Measurements

1 24 inches = ____ feet

2 4 meters = ____ centimeters

3 5 yards = ____ feet

4 $1\frac{1}{2}$ feet = ____ inches

5 2 kilometers = ____ meters

6 9 feet = ____ yards

7 2.5 meters = ____ centimeters

8 $\frac{3}{4}$ meter = ____ millimeters

9 $\frac{1}{4}$ mile = ____ yards

10 10 millimeters = ____ centimeter

Equivalent Measurements

1 $\frac{1}{2}$ cup = ⬚ ounces

2 3 deciliters = ⬚ centiliters

3 $1\frac{1}{2}$ quarts = ⬚ pints

4 $1\frac{1}{2}$ centiliters = ⬚ milliliters

5 1 pint = ⬚ ounces

6 4 cups = ⬚ pints

7 2 liters = ⬚ milliliters

8 $2\frac{1}{4}$ gallons = ⬚ quarts

9 50 deciliters = ⬚ liters

10 1 liter = ⬚ centiliters

Measurement Charts
Length

U.S. Customary

12 inches = 1 foot

3 feet = 1 yard

5,280 feet = 1 mile

1,760 yards = 1 mile

Metric

10 millimeters (mm) = 1 centimeter (cm)

10 centimeters = 1 decimeter (dm)

10 decimeters = 1 meter (m)

1,000 meters = 1 kilometer (km)

2	400	1	<u>6</u>	18	2,000
3	250	750	15	440	36
4	4	30	2,000	3	15
16	5	1,000	2	<u>9</u>	100

Measurement Charts
Capacity

U.S. Customary

8 ounces = 1 cup

2 cups = 1 pint

2 pints = 1 quart

4 quarts = 1 gallon

Metric

10 milliliters (ml) = 1 centiliter (cl)

10 centiliters = 1 deciliter (dl)

10 deciliters = 1 liter (l)

Equivalent Measurements • EMC 3075 • © Evan-Moor Corp.

Equivalent
Measurements

EMC 3075
© Evan-Moor Corp.

Equivalent
Measurements

EMC 3075
© Evan-Moor Corp.

Equivalent
Measurements

EMC 3075
© Evan-Moor Corp.

Equivalent
Measurements

EMC 3075
© Evan-Moor Corp.

Equivalent
Measurements

EMC 3075
© Evan-Moor Corp.

Equivalent
Measurements

EMC 3075
© Evan-Moor Corp.

Equivalent
Measurements

EMC 3075
© Evan-Moor Corp.

Equivalent
Measurements

EMC 3075
© Evan-Moor Corp.

Equivalent
Measurements

EMC 3075
© Evan-Moor Corp.

Equivalent
Measurements

EMC 3075
© Evan-Moor Corp.

Equivalent
Measurements

EMC 3075
© Evan-Moor Corp.

Equivalent
Measurements

EMC 3075
© Evan-Moor Corp.

Equivalent
Measurements

EMC 3075
© Evan-Moor Corp.

Equivalent
Measurements

EMC 3075
© Evan-Moor Corp.

Equivalent
Measurements

EMC 3075
© Evan-Moor Corp.

Equivalent
Measurements

EMC 3075
© Evan-Moor Corp.

Equivalent
Measurements

EMC 3075
© Evan-Moor Corp.

Equivalent
Measurements

EMC 3075
© Evan-Moor Corp.

Equivalent
Measurements

EMC 3075
© Evan-Moor Corp.

Equivalent
Measurements

EMC 3075
© Evan-Moor Corp.

Equivalent
Measurements

EMC 3075
© Evan-Moor Corp.

Equivalent
Measurements

EMC 3075
© Evan-Moor Corp.

Equivalent
Measurements

EMC 3075
© Evan-Moor Corp.

Equivalent
Measurements

EMC 3075
© Evan-Moor Corp.

Plot It!

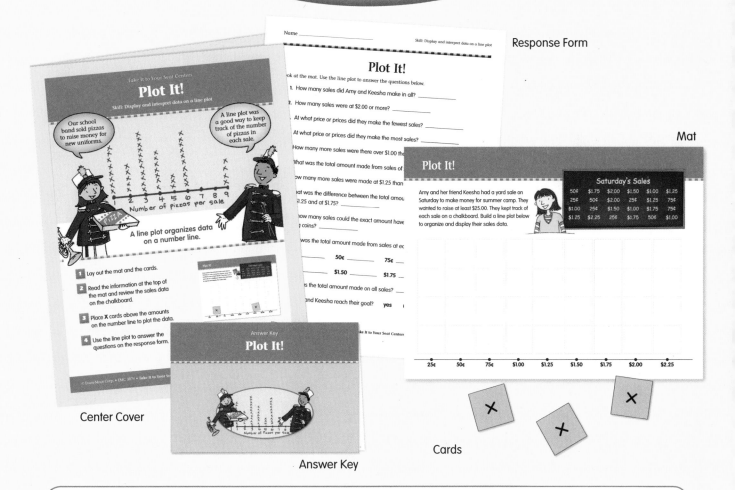

Response Form

Mat

Center Cover

Answer Key

Cards

Skill: Display and interpret data on a line plot

Steps to Follow

1. **Prepare the center.** (See page 3.)

2. **Introduce the center.** State the goal. Say: *You will build a line plot and answer questions about the data.*

3. **Teach the skill.** Demonstrate how to use the center with individual students or small groups.

4. **Practice the skill.** Have students use the center independently or with a partner.

Contents

Plot It!

Look at the mat. Use the line plot to answer the questions below.

1. How many sales did Amy and Keesha make in all? _____

2. How many sales were at $2.00 or more? _____

3. At what price or prices did they make the fewest sales? _____

4. At what price or prices did they make the most sales? _____

5. How many more sales were there over $1.00 than under $1.00? _____

6. What was the total amount made from sales of $1.00 or more? _____

7. How many more sales were made at $1.25 than at $2.25? _____

8. What was the difference between the total amount made from sales at $1.25 and at $1.75? _____

9. For how many sales could the exact amount have been paid without using coins? _____

10. What was the total amount made from sales at each price below?

    25¢ _____   50¢ _____   75¢ _____ $1.00 _____

    $1.25 _____ $1.50 _____ $1.75 _____ $2.00 _____

11. What was the total amount made on all sales? _____

12. Did Amy and Keesha reach their goal?   **yes**   **no**

Plot It!

Skill: Display and interpret data on a line plot

Our school band sold pizzas to raise money for new uniforms.

A line plot was a good way to keep track of the number of pizzas in each sale.

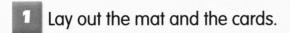
Number of Pizzas per Sale

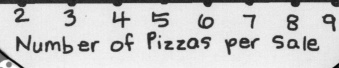
A line plot organizes data on a number line.

1. Lay out the mat and the cards.

2. Read the information at the top of the mat and review the sales data on the chalkboard.

3. Place **X** cards above the amounts on the number line to plot the data.

4. Use the line plot to answer the questions on the response form.

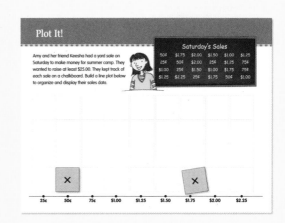

Response Form

Plot It!

Look at the mat. Use the line plot to answer the questions below.

1. How many sales did Amy and Keesha make in all? __24__

2. How many sales were at $2.00 or more? __3__

3. At what price or prices did they make the fewest sales? __$2.25__

4. At what price or prices did they make the most sales? __25¢ and $1.00__

5. How many more sales were there over $1.00 than under $1.00? __2__

6. What was the total amount made from sales of $1.00 or more? __$22.25__

7. How many more sales were made at $1.25 than at $2.25? __2__

8. What was the difference between the total amount made from sales at $1.25 and at $1.75? __$1.50__

9. For how many sales could the exact amount have been paid without using coins? __6__

10. What was the total amount made from sales at each price below?

25¢	$1.00	50¢	$1.50	75¢	$1.50	$1.00	$4.00
$1.25	$3.75	$1.50	$3.00	$1.75	$5.25	$2.00	$2.00	$4.00

11. What was the total amount made on all sales? __$26.25__

12. Did Amy and Keesha reach their goal? (yes) no

Answer Key

Plot It!

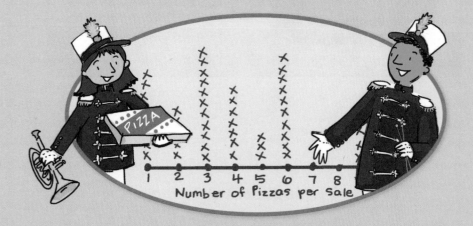

Number of Pizzas per Sale

Plot It!

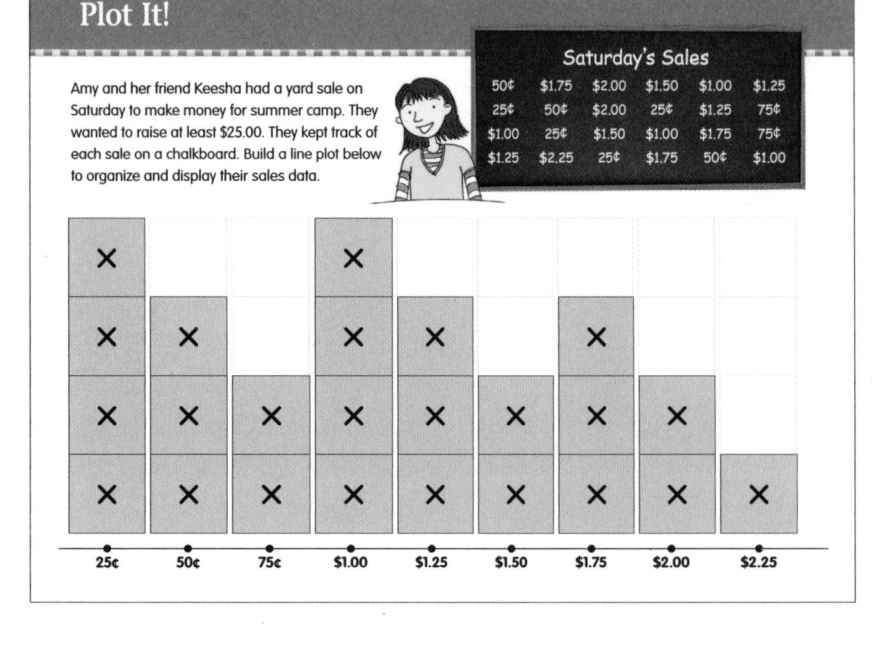

Plot It!

Amy and her friend Keesha had a yard sale on Saturday to make money for summer camp. They wanted to raise at least $25.00. They kept track of each sale on a chalkboard. Build a line plot below to organize and display their sales data.

Saturday's Sales

50¢	$1.75	$2.00	$1.50	$1.00	$1.25
25¢		50¢	$2.00	25¢	75¢
$1.00		25¢	$1.50	$1.00	75¢
$1.25		$2.25	25¢	$1.75	$1.00
				50¢	

25¢   50¢   75¢ $1.00 $1.25 $1.50 $1.75 $2.00 $2.25

Plot It! **EMC 3075** © Evan-Moor Corp.	**Plot It!** **EMC 3075** © Evan-Moor Corp.	**Plot It!** **EMC 3075** © Evan-Moor Corp.	**Plot It!** **EMC 3075** © Evan-Moor Corp.	**Plot It!** **EMC 3075** © Evan-Moor Corp.	**Plot It!** **EMC 3075** © Evan-Moor Corp.
Plot It! **EMC 3075** © Evan-Moor Corp.	**Plot It!** **EMC 3075** © Evan-Moor Corp.	**Plot It!** **EMC 3075** © Evan-Moor Corp.	**Plot It!** **EMC 3075** © Evan-Moor Corp.	**Plot It!** **EMC 3075** © Evan-Moor Corp.	**Plot It!** **EMC 3075** © Evan-Moor Corp.
Plot It! **EMC 3075** © Evan-Moor Corp.	**Plot It!** **EMC 3075** © Evan-Moor Corp.	**Plot It!** **EMC 3075** © Evan-Moor Corp.	**Plot It!** **EMC 3075** © Evan-Moor Corp.	**Plot It!** **EMC 3075** © Evan-Moor Corp.	**Plot It!** **EMC 3075** © Evan-Moor Corp.
Plot It! **EMC 3075** © Evan-Moor Corp.	**Plot It!** **EMC 3075** © Evan-Moor Corp.	**Plot It!** **EMC 3075** © Evan-Moor Corp.	**Plot It!** **EMC 3075** © Evan-Moor Corp.	**Plot It!** **EMC 3075** © Evan-Moor Corp.	**Plot It!** **EMC 3075** © Evan-Moor Corp.
Plot It! **EMC 3075** © Evan-Moor Corp.	**Plot It!** **EMC 3075** © Evan-Moor Corp.	**Plot It!** **EMC 3075** © Evan-Moor Corp.	**Plot It!** **EMC 3075** © Evan-Moor Corp.	**Plot It!** **EMC 3075** © Evan-Moor Corp.	**Plot It!** **EMC 3075** © Evan-Moor Corp.
Plot It! **EMC 3075** © Evan-Moor Corp.	**Plot It!** **EMC 3075** © Evan-Moor Corp.	**Plot It!** **EMC 3075** © Evan-Moor Corp.	**Plot It!** **EMC 3075** © Evan-Moor Corp.	**Plot It!** **EMC 3075** © Evan-Moor Corp.	**Plot It!** **EMC 3075** © Evan-Moor Corp.

Measures of Center

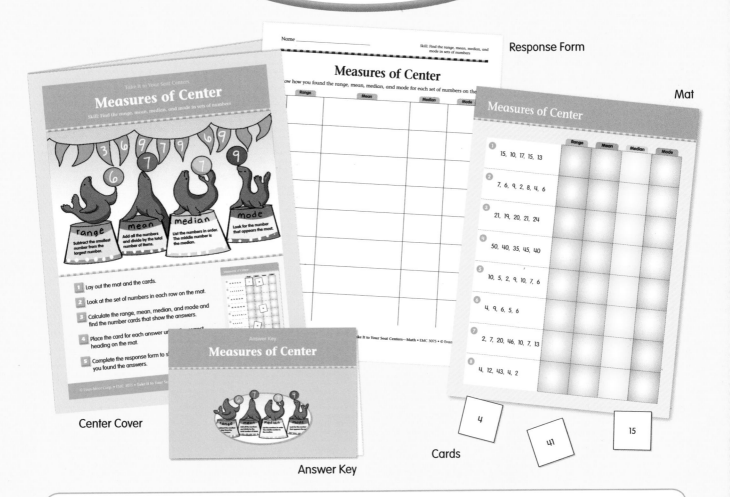

Response Form

Mat

Center Cover

Answer Key

Cards

Skill: Find the range, mean, median, and mode in sets of numbers

Steps to Follow

1. **Prepare the center.** (See page 3.)

2. **Introduce the center.** State the goal. Say: *You will find the range, mean, median, and mode for each set of numbers on the mat.*

3. **Teach the skill.** Demonstrate how to use the center with individual students or small groups.

4. **Practice the skill.** Have students use the center independently or with a partner.

Contents

Measures of Center

Show how you found the range, mean, median, and mode for each set of numbers on the mat.

	Range	Mean	Median	Mode
1				
2				
3				
4				
5				
6				
7				
8				

Measures of Center

Skill: Find the range, mean, median, and mode in sets of numbers

range
Subtract the smallest number from the largest number.

mean
Add all the numbers and divide by the total number of items.

median
List the numbers in order. The middle number is the median.

mode
Look for the number that appears the most.

1 Lay out the mat and the cards.

2 Look at the set of numbers in each row on the mat.

3 Calculate the range, mean, median, and mode and find the number cards that show the answers.

4 Place the card for each answer under the correct heading on the mat.

5 Complete the response form to show how you found the answers.

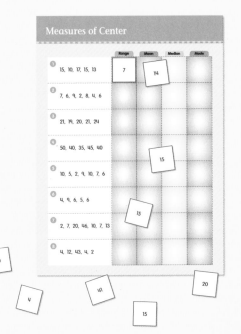

Response Form

Measures of Center

Show how you found the range, mean, median, and mode for each set of numbers on the mat.

	Range	Mean	Median	Mode
1	17 − 10 = 7	15 + 10 + 17 + 15 + 13 = 70 70 ÷ 5 = 14	10, 13, **15**, 15, 17	**15**, 10, 17, **15**, 13
2	9 − 2 = 7	7 + 6 + 4 + 2 + 8 + 9 + 6 = 42 42 ÷ 7 = 6	2, 4, 6, **6**, 7, 8, 9	7, **6**, 4, 2, 8, 9, **6**
3	24 − 19 = 5	21 + 19 + 20 + 21 + 24 = 105 105 ÷ 5 = 21	19, 20, **21**, 21, 24	**21**, 19, 20, **21**, 24
4	50 − 35 = 15	50 + 40 + 35 + 45 + 40 = 210 210 ÷ 5 = 42	35, **40**, 40, 45, 50	50, **40**, 35, 45, **40**
5	10 − 2 = 8	10 + 5 + 2 + 9 + 10 + 7 + 6 = 49 49 ÷ 7 = 7	2, 5, 6, **7**, 9, 10, 10	**10**, 5, 2, 9, **10**, 7, 6
6	9 − 4 = 5	4 + 9 + 6 + 5 + 6 = 30 30 ÷ 5 = 6	4, 5, **6**, 6, 9	4, 9, **6**, 5, **6**
7	46 − 2 = 44	2 + 7 + 20 + 46 + 10 + 7 + 13 = 105 105 ÷ 7 = 15	2, 7, 7, **10**, 13, 20, 46	2, **7**, 20, 46, 10, **7**, 13
8	43 − 2 = 41	4 + 12 + 43 + 4 + 2 = 65 65 ÷ 5 = 13	2, **4**, 4, 12, 43	**4**, 12, 43, **4**, 2

(fold)

Answer Key

Measures of Center

range — Subtract the smallest number from the largest number.

mean — Add all the numbers and divide by the total number of items.

median — List the numbers in order. The middle number is the median.

mode — Look for the number that appears the most.

Measures of Center

Measures of Center

	Range	Mean	Median	Mode
1. 15, 10, 17, 15, 13	7	14	15	15
2. 7, 6, 9, 2, 8, 4, 6	7	6̄	6̄	6̄
3. 21, 19, 20, 21, 24	5	21	21	21
4. 50, 40, 35, 45, 40	15	42	40	40
5. 10, 5, 2, 9, 10, 7, 6	8	7	7	10
6. 4, 9, 6, 5, 6	5	6̄	6̄	6̄
7. 2, 7, 20, 46, 10, 7, 13	44	15	10	7
8. 4, 12, 43, 4, 2	41	13	4	4

Measures of Center

	Range	Mean	Median	Mode
1 15, 10, 17, 15, 13				
2 7, 6, 9, 2, 8, 4, 6				
3 21, 19, 20, 21, 24				
4 50, 40, 35, 45, 40				
5 10, 5, 2, 9, 10, 7, 6				
6 4, 9, 6, 5, 6				
7 2, 7, 20, 46, 10, 7, 13				
8 4, 12, 43, 4, 2				

2	2	2	2	4	4	4
4	5	5	<u>6</u>	<u>6</u>	<u>6</u>	<u>6</u>
<u>6</u>	<u>6</u>	7	7	7	7	7
8	<u>9</u>	<u>9</u>	<u>9</u>	10	10	10
10	12	13	13	14	14	15
15	15	15	17	19	20	20
21	21	21	24	35	40	40
41	42	43	44	45	46	50

Measures of Center EMC 3075 © Evan-Moor Corp.	Measures of Center EMC 3075 © Evan-Moor Corp.	Measures of Center EMC 3075 © Evan-Moor Corp.	Measures of Center EMC 3075 © Evan-Moor Corp.	Measures of Center EMC 3075 © Evan-Moor Corp.	Measures of Center EMC 3075 © Evan-Moor Corp.	Measures of Center EMC 3075 © Evan-Moor Corp.
Measures of Center EMC 3075 © Evan-Moor Corp.	Measures of Center EMC 3075 © Evan-Moor Corp.	Measures of Center EMC 3075 © Evan-Moor Corp.	Measures of Center EMC 3075 © Evan-Moor Corp.	Measures of Center EMC 3075 © Evan-Moor Corp.	Measures of Center EMC 3075 © Evan-Moor Corp.	Measures of Center EMC 3075 © Evan-Moor Corp.
Measures of Center EMC 3075 © Evan-Moor Corp.	Measures of Center EMC 3075 © Evan-Moor Corp.	Measures of Center EMC 3075 © Evan-Moor Corp.	Measures of Center EMC 3075 © Evan-Moor Corp.	Measures of Center EMC 3075 © Evan-Moor Corp.	Measures of Center EMC 3075 © Evan-Moor Corp.	Measures of Center EMC 3075 © Evan-Moor Corp.
Measures of Center EMC 3075 © Evan-Moor Corp.	Measures of Center EMC 3075 © Evan-Moor Corp.	Measures of Center EMC 3075 © Evan-Moor Corp.	Measures of Center EMC 3075 © Evan-Moor Corp.	Measures of Center EMC 3075 © Evan-Moor Corp.	Measures of Center EMC 3075 © Evan-Moor Corp.	Measures of Center EMC 3075 © Evan-Moor Corp.
Measures of Center EMC 3075 © Evan-Moor Corp.	Measures of Center EMC 3075 © Evan-Moor Corp.	Measures of Center EMC 3075 © Evan-Moor Corp.	Measures of Center EMC 3075 © Evan-Moor Corp.	Measures of Center EMC 3075 © Evan-Moor Corp.	Measures of Center EMC 3075 © Evan-Moor Corp.	Measures of Center EMC 3075 © Evan-Moor Corp.
Measures of Center EMC 3075 © Evan-Moor Corp.	Measures of Center EMC 3075 © Evan-Moor Corp.	Measures of Center EMC 3075 © Evan-Moor Corp.	Measures of Center EMC 3075 © Evan-Moor Corp.	Measures of Center EMC 3075 © Evan-Moor Corp.	Measures of Center EMC 3075 © Evan-Moor Corp.	Measures of Center EMC 3075 © Evan-Moor Corp.
Measures of Center EMC 3075 © Evan-Moor Corp.	Measures of Center EMC 3075 © Evan-Moor Corp.	Measures of Center EMC 3075 © Evan-Moor Corp.	Measures of Center EMC 3075 © Evan-Moor Corp.	Measures of Center EMC 3075 © Evan-Moor Corp.	Measures of Center EMC 3075 © Evan-Moor Corp.	Measures of Center EMC 3075 © Evan-Moor Corp.
Measures of Center EMC 3075 © Evan-Moor Corp.	Measures of Center EMC 3075 © Evan-Moor Corp.	Measures of Center EMC 3075 © Evan-Moor Corp.	Measures of Center EMC 3075 © Evan-Moor Corp.	Measures of Center EMC 3075 © Evan-Moor Corp.	Measures of Center EMC 3075 © Evan-Moor Corp.	Measures of Center EMC 3075 © Evan-Moor Corp.

Volume

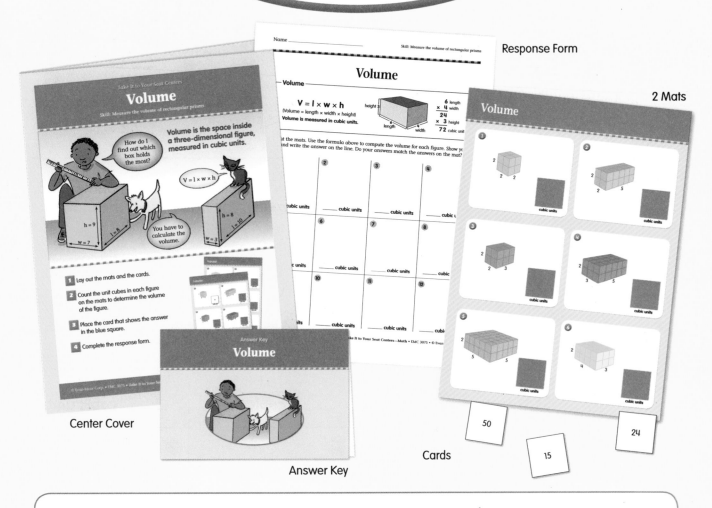

Center Cover

Answer Key

Response Form

Cards

2 Mats

Skill: Measure the volume of rectangular prisms by counting unit cubes and by applying the formula $V = l \times w \times h$

Steps to Follow

1. **Prepare the center.** (See page 3.)

2. **Introduce the center.** State the goal. Say: *You will find the volume of each figure on the mats by counting unit cubes and by applying a formula.*

3. **Teach the skill.** Demonstrate how to use the center with individual students or small groups.

4. **Practice the skill.** Have students use the center independently or with a partner.

Contents

Volume

┌ Volume ─────────────────────

$$V = l \times w \times h$$

(Volume = length × width × height)

Volume is measured in cubic units.

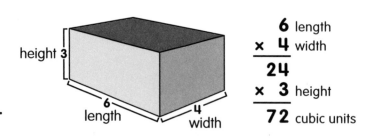

height 3

6 length

4 width

$$\begin{array}{r} 6 \text{ length} \\ \times\ 4 \text{ width} \\ \hline 24 \\ \times\ 3 \text{ height} \\ \hline 72 \text{ cubic units} \end{array}$$

Look at the mats. Use the formula above to compute the volume for each figure. Show your work and write the answer on the line. Do your answers match the answers on the mat?

1	**2**	**3**	**4**
_____ cubic units	_____ cubic units	_____ cubic units	_____ cubic units
5	**6**	**7**	**8**
_____ cubic units	_____ cubic units	_____ cubic units	_____ cubic units
9	**10**	**11**	**12**
_____ cubic units	_____ cubic units	_____ cubic units	_____ cubic units

Volume

Skill: Measure the volume of rectangular prisms

How do I find out which box holds the most?

Volume is the space inside a three-dimensional figure, measured in cubic units.

$V = l \times w \times h$

h = 9
l = 8
w = 7

You have to calculate the volume.

h = 8
l = 10
w = 3

1 Lay out the mats and the cards.

2 Count the unit cubes in each figure on the mats to determine the volume of the figure.

3 Place the card that shows the answer in the blue square.

4 Complete the response form.

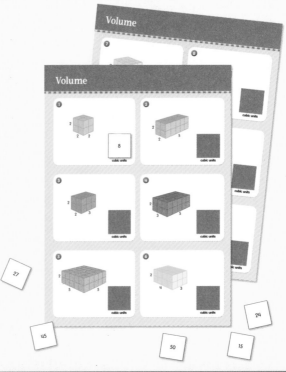

(fold)

Response Form

Volume

Volume

$$V = l \times w \times h$$

(Volume = length × width × height)

Volume is measured in cubic units.

height 3

6 length
× 4 width
24
× 3 height
72 cubic units

length 6   width 4

Look at the mats. Use the formula above to compute the volume for each figure. Show your work and write the answer on the line. Do your answers match the answers on the mat?

1	2	**2**	5	
	× 2		× 2	
	4		10	
	× 2		× 2	
	8		20	
	8 cubic units		20 cubic units	

1. 2
    × 2
    4
    × 2
    8
    __8__ cubic units

2. 5
    × 2
    10
    × 2
    20
    __20__ cubic units

3. 3
    × 2
    6
    × 2
    12
    __12__ cubic units

4. 5
    × 3
    15
    × 2
    30
    __30__ cubic units

5. 5
    × 5
    25
    × 2
    50
    __50__ cubic units

6. 4
    × 3
    12
    × 2
    24
    __24__ cubic units

7. 3
    × 3
    9
    × 2
    18
    __18__ cubic units

8. 3
    × 3
    9
    × 3
    27
    __27__ cubic units

9. 5
    × 4
    20
    × 3
    60
    __60__ cubic units

10. 5
    × 3
    15
    × 3
    45
    __45__ cubic units

11. 5
    × 4
    20
    × 4
    80
    __80__ cubic units

12. 5
    × 3
    15
    × 5
    75
    __75__ cubic units

Volume

Volume

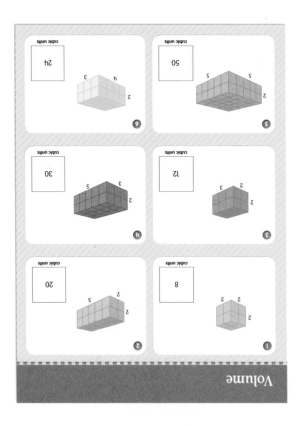

Volume

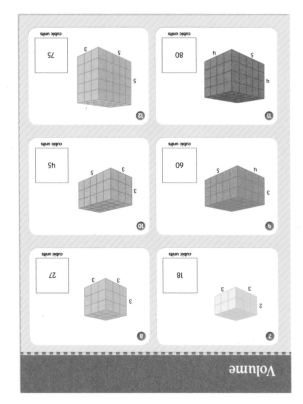

Volume

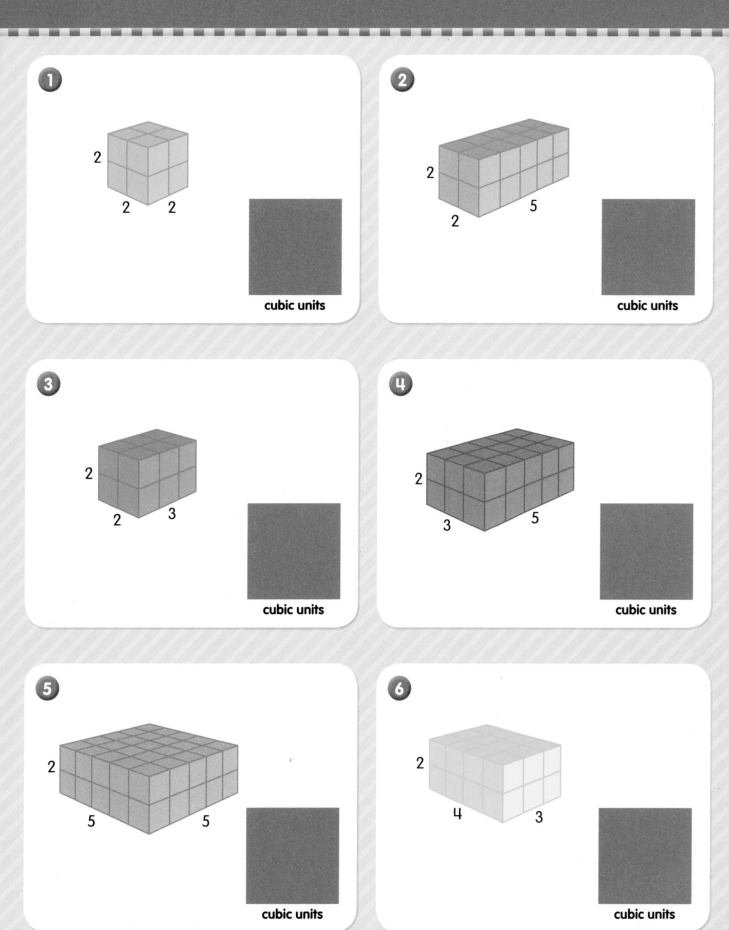

1

2
2   2

cubic units

2

2
2   5

cubic units

3

2
2   3

cubic units

4

2
3   5

cubic units

5

2
5   5

cubic units

6

2
4   3

cubic units

Volume

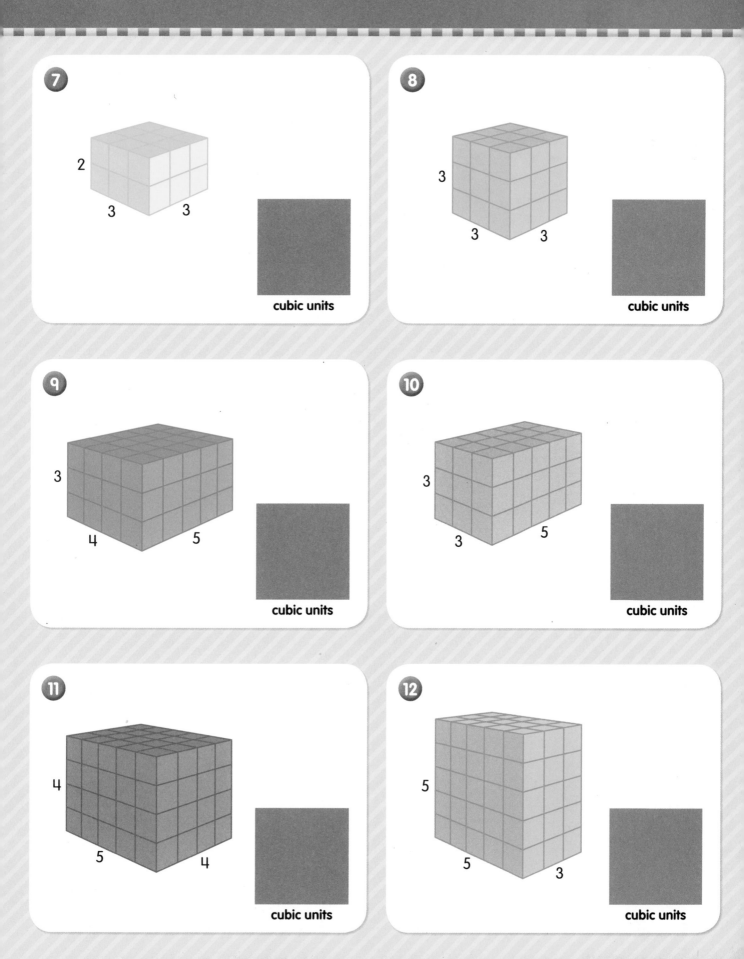

7

2
3
3

cubic units

8

3
3
3

cubic units

9

3
4
5

cubic units

10

3
3
5

cubic units

11

4
5
4

cubic units

12

5
5
3

cubic units

8	10	12	15	17	18
20	22	24	27	29	30
38	40	42	45	47	48
50	52	54	57	59	60
68	70	72	75	77	78
80	82	84	87	89	90

Volume	Volume	Volume	Volume	Volume	Volume
EMC 3075	**EMC 3075**	**EMC 3075**	**EMC 3075**	**EMC 3075**	**EMC 3075**
© Evan-Moor Corp.	© Evan-Moor Corp.	© Evan-Moor Corp.	© Evan-Moor Corp.	© Evan-Moor Corp.	© Evan-Moor Corp.
Volume	Volume	Volume	Volume	Volume	Volume
EMC 3075	**EMC 3075**	**EMC 3075**	**EMC 3075**	**EMC 3075**	**EMC 3075**
© Evan-Moor Corp.	© Evan-Moor Corp.	© Evan-Moor Corp.	© Evan-Moor Corp.	© Evan-Moor Corp.	© Evan-Moor Corp.
Volume	Volume	Volume	Volume	Volume	Volume
EMC 3075	**EMC 3075**	**EMC 3075**	**EMC 3075**	**EMC 3075**	**EMC 3075**
© Evan-Moor Corp.	© Evan-Moor Corp.	© Evan-Moor Corp.	© Evan-Moor Corp.	© Evan-Moor Corp.	© Evan-Moor Corp.
Volume	Volume	Volume	Volume	Volume	Volume
EMC 3075	**EMC 3075**	**EMC 3075**	**EMC 3075**	**EMC 3075**	**EMC 3075**
© Evan-Moor Corp.	© Evan-Moor Corp.	© Evan-Moor Corp.	© Evan-Moor Corp.	© Evan-Moor Corp.	© Evan-Moor Corp.
Volume	Volume	Volume	Volume	Volume	Volume
EMC 3075	**EMC 3075**	**EMC 3075**	**EMC 3075**	**EMC 3075**	**EMC 3075**
© Evan-Moor Corp.	© Evan-Moor Corp.	© Evan-Moor Corp.	© Evan-Moor Corp.	© Evan-Moor Corp.	© Evan-Moor Corp.
Volume	Volume	Volume	Volume	Volume	Volume
EMC 3075	**EMC 3075**	**EMC 3075**	**EMC 3075**	**EMC 3075**	**EMC 3075**
© Evan-Moor Corp.	© Evan-Moor Corp.	© Evan-Moor Corp.	© Evan-Moor Corp.	© Evan-Moor Corp.	© Evan-Moor Corp.

What Is the Chance?

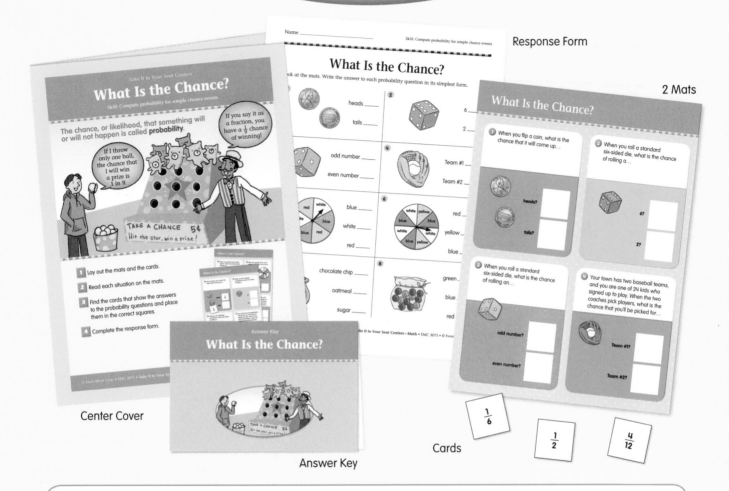

Response Form

2 Mats

Center Cover

Answer Key

Cards

Skill: Compute probability for simple chance events

Steps to Follow

1. **Prepare the center.** (See page 3.)

2. **Introduce the center.** State the goal. Say: *You will determine the probability of different outcomes for each situation on the mats.*

3. **Teach the skill.** Demonstrate how to use the center with individual students or small groups.

4. **Practice the skill.** Have students use the center independently or with a partner.

Contents

What Is the Chance?

Look at the mats. Write the answer to each probability question in its simplest form.

1

heads _____

tails _____

2

6 _____

2 _____

3

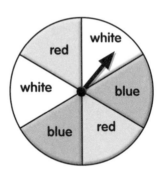

odd number _____

even number _____

4

green

Team #1 _____

Team #2 _____

5

blue _____

white _____

red _____

6

red _____

yellow _____

blue _____

7

chocolate chip _____

oatmeal _____

sugar _____

8

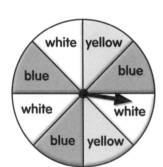

green _____

blue _____

red _____

What Is the Chance?

Skill: Compute probability for simple chance events

The chance, or likelihood, that something will or will not happen is called **probability**.

If I throw only one ball, the chance that I will win a prize is 1 in 9.

If you say it as a fraction, you have a $\frac{1}{9}$ chance of winning!

TAKE A CHANCE 5¢
Hit the star, win a prize!

1 Lay out the mats and the cards.

2 Read each situation on the mats.

3 Find the cards that show the answers to the probability questions and place them in the correct squares.

4 Complete the response form.

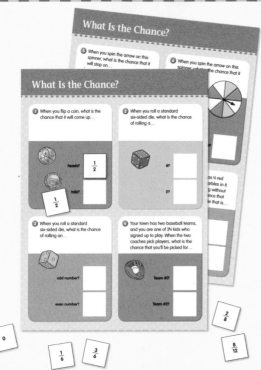

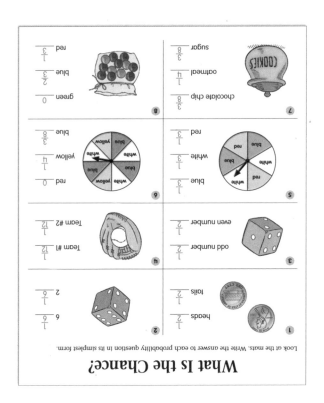

Response Form

(fold)

What Is the Chance?

Look at the mats. Write the answer to each probability question in its simplest form.

1. heads $\frac{1}{2}$ tails $\frac{1}{2}$

2. 6 $\frac{1}{6}$ 2 $\frac{1}{6}$

3. odd number $\frac{1}{2}$ even number $\frac{1}{2}$

4. Team #1 $\frac{1}{12}$ Team #2 $\frac{1}{12}$

5. blue $\frac{1}{3}$ white $\frac{1}{3}$ red $\frac{1}{3}$

6. red 0 yellow $\frac{1}{4}$ blue $\frac{3}{8}$

7. chocolate chip $\frac{3}{8}$ oatmeal $\frac{1}{4}$ sugar $\frac{3}{8}$

8. green 0 blue $\frac{2}{3}$ red $\frac{1}{3}$

Answer Key

What Is the Chance?

TAKE A CHANCE 5¢
Hit the star, win a prize!

Answer Key

What Is the Chance?

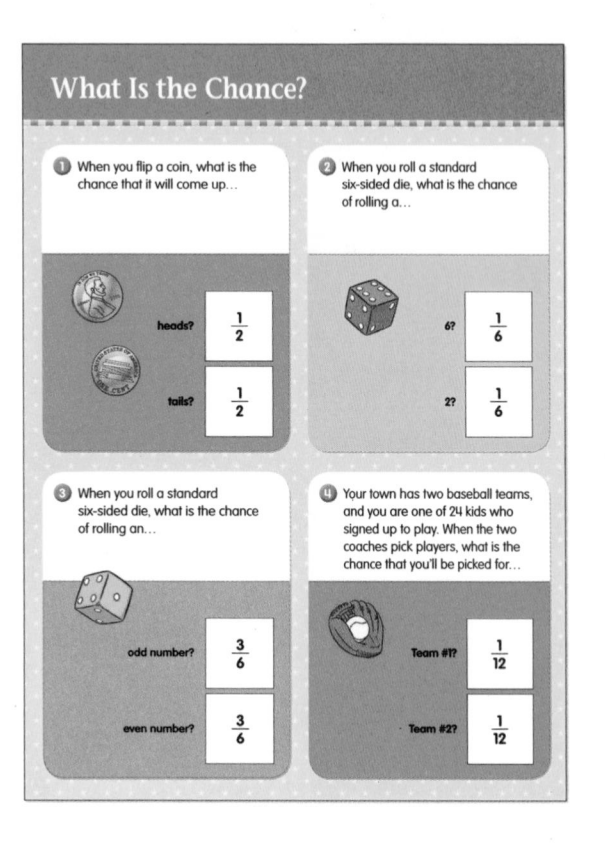

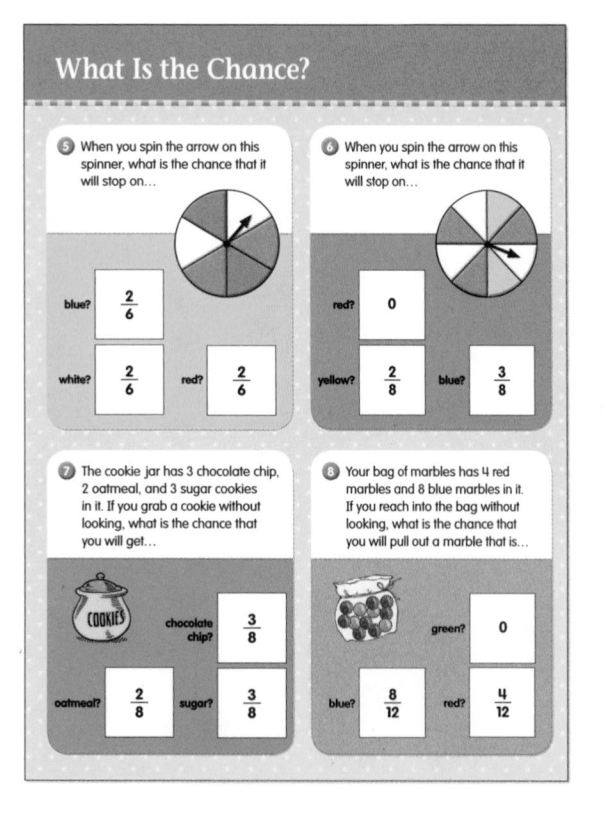

What Is the Chance?

1 When you flip a coin, what is the chance that it will come up…

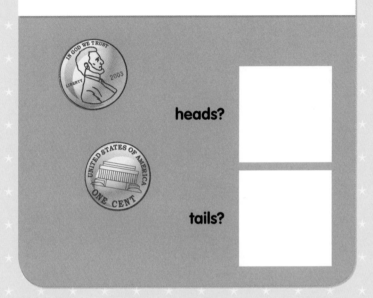

heads?

tails?

2 When you roll a standard six-sided die, what is the chance of rolling a…

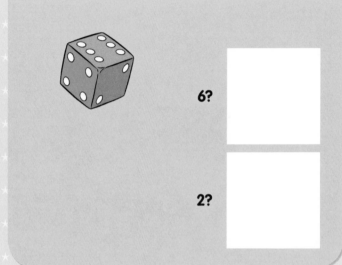

6?

2?

3 When you roll a standard six-sided die, what is the chance of rolling an…

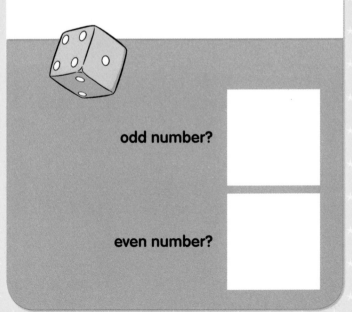

odd number?

even number?

4 Your town has two baseball teams, and you are one of 24 kids who signed up to play. When the two coaches pick players, what is the chance that you'll be picked for…

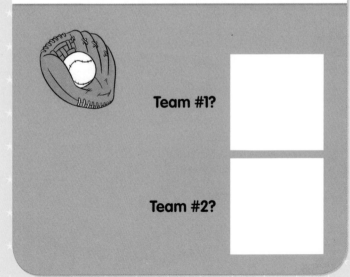

Team #1?

Team #2?

What Is the Chance?

5 When you spin the arrow on this spinner, what is the chance that it will stop on…

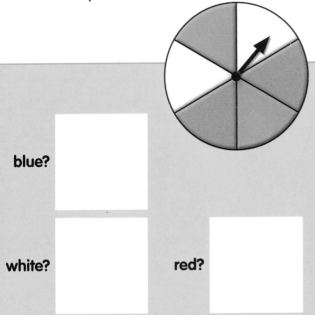

blue?

white?

red?

6 When you spin the arrow on this spinner, what is the chance that it will stop on…

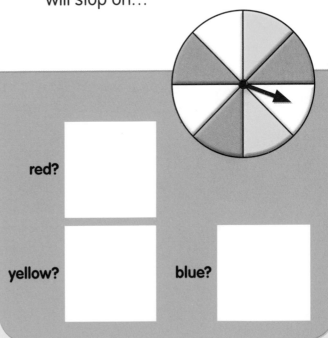

red?

yellow?

blue?

7 The cookie jar has 3 chocolate chip, 2 oatmeal, and 3 sugar cookies in it. If you grab a cookie without looking, what is the chance that you will get…

chocolate chip?

oatmeal?

sugar?

8 Your bag of marbles has 4 red marbles and 8 blue marbles in it. If you reach into the bag without looking, what is the chance that you will pull out a marble that is…

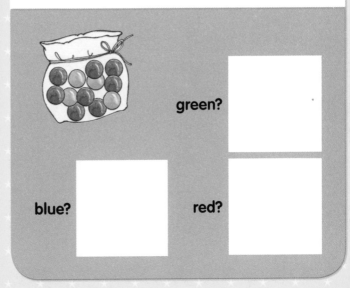

green?

blue?

red?

$\dfrac{4}{12}$	$\dfrac{8}{12}$	0	$\dfrac{2}{8}$
$\dfrac{3}{8}$	$\dfrac{3}{8}$	$\dfrac{2}{8}$	$\dfrac{3}{8}$
0	$\dfrac{2}{6}$	$\dfrac{2}{6}$	$\dfrac{2}{6}$
$\dfrac{4}{12}$	$\dfrac{8}{12}$	0	$\dfrac{1}{2}$
$\dfrac{1}{2}$	$\dfrac{1}{6}$	$\dfrac{1}{6}$	$\dfrac{1}{12}$
0	$\dfrac{3}{6}$	$\dfrac{3}{6}$	$\dfrac{1}{12}$

What Is the Chance? **EMC 3075** © Evan-Moor Corp.	What Is the Chance? **EMC 3075** © Evan-Moor Corp.	What Is the Chance? **EMC 3075** © Evan-Moor Corp.	What Is the Chance? **EMC 3075** © Evan-Moor Corp.
What Is the Chance? **EMC 3075** © Evan-Moor Corp.	What Is the Chance? **EMC 3075** © Evan-Moor Corp.	What Is the Chance? **EMC 3075** © Evan-Moor Corp.	What Is the Chance? **EMC 3075** © Evan-Moor Corp.
What Is the Chance? **EMC 3075** © Evan-Moor Corp.	What Is the Chance? **EMC 3075** © Evan-Moor Corp.	What Is the Chance? **EMC 3075** © Evan-Moor Corp.	What Is the Chance? **EMC 3075** © Evan-Moor Corp.
What Is the Chance? **EMC 3075** © Evan-Moor Corp.	What Is the Chance? **EMC 3075** © Evan-Moor Corp.	What Is the Chance? **EMC 3075** © Evan-Moor Corp.	What Is the Chance? **EMC 3075** © Evan-Moor Corp.
What Is the Chance? **EMC 3075** © Evan-Moor Corp.	What Is the Chance? **EMC 3075** © Evan-Moor Corp.	What Is the Chance? **EMC 3075** © Evan-Moor Corp.	What Is the Chance? **EMC 3075** © Evan-Moor Corp.
What Is the Chance? **EMC 3075** © Evan-Moor Corp.	What Is the Chance? **EMC 3075** © Evan-Moor Corp.	What Is the Chance? **EMC 3075** © Evan-Moor Corp.	What Is the Chance? **EMC 3075** © Evan-Moor Corp.

Math Terms

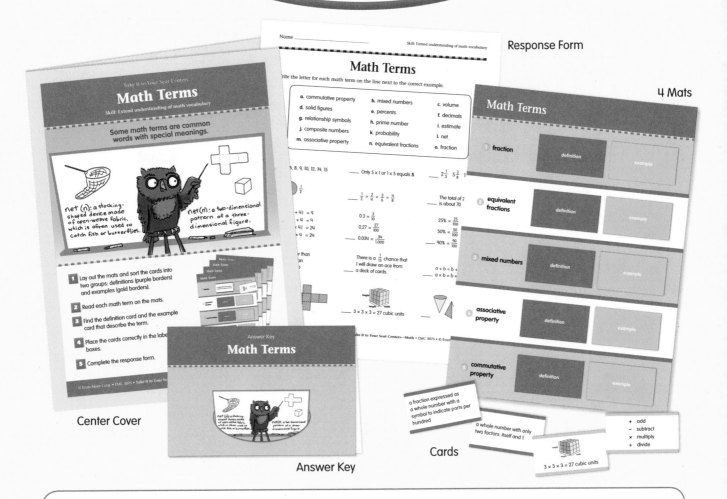

Response Form

4 Mats

Center Cover

Answer Key

Cards

Skill: Extend understanding of math vocabulary

Steps to Follow

1. **Prepare the center.** (See page 3.)

2. **Introduce the center.** State the goal. Say:
   You will find the correct definition and example cards for each math term on the mats.

3. **Teach the skill.** Demonstrate how to use the center with individual students or small groups.

4. **Practice the skill.** Have students use the center independently or with a partner.

Contents

Math Terms

Write the letter for each math term on the line next to the correct example.

---

a. commutative property   **b.** mixed numbers   **c.** volume

d. solid figures   **e.** percents   **f.** decimals

g. relationship symbols   **h.** prime number   **i.** estimate

j. composite numbers   **k.** probability   **l.** net

m. associative property   **n.** equivalent fractions **o.** fraction

---

____ 4, 6, 8, 9, 10, 12, 14, 15

____ Only 5 x 1 or 1 x 5 equals **5**.

____ $2\frac{1}{3}$ $5\frac{3}{8}$ $1\frac{4}{5}$

____ $\frac{1}{2}$

____ $\frac{1}{2} = \frac{2}{4} = \frac{3}{6} = \frac{4}{8}$

____ The total of 23 + 46 is about 70.

$2 + (3 + 4) = 9$
$(2 + 3) + 4 = 9$
$2 \times (3 \times 4) = 24$
____ $(2 \times 3) \times 4 = 24$

$0.3 = \frac{3}{10}$
$0.27 = \frac{27}{100}$
____ $0.034 = \frac{34}{1,000}$

$25\% = \frac{25}{100}$
$50\% = \frac{50}{100}$
____ $90\% = \frac{90}{100}$

> greater than
< less than
____ = equal to

There is a $\frac{1}{13}$ chance that
I will draw an ace from
____ a deck of cards.

$a + b = b + a$
____ $a \times b = b \times a$

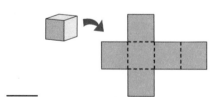

____

____ 3 x 3 x 3 = 27 cubic units

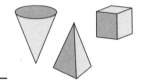

____

Math Terms

Skill: Extend understanding of math vocabulary

Some math terms are common words with special meanings.

net (n): a stocking-shaped device made of open-weave fabric, which is often used to catch fish or butterflies.

net (n): a two-dimensional pattern of a three-dimensional figure.

1 Lay out the mats and sort the cards into two groups: definitions (purple borders) and examples (gold borders).

2 Read each math term on the mats.

3 Find the definition card and the example card that describe the term.

4 Place the cards correctly in the labeled boxes.

5 Complete the response form.

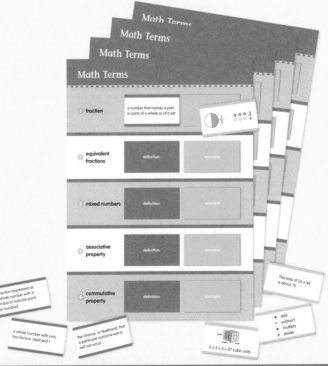

Net (n): a stocking-shaped device made of open-weave fabric, which is often used to catch fish or butterflies.

Net (n): a two-dimensional pattern of a three-dimensional figure.

Math Terms

Answer Key

(fold)

Response Form

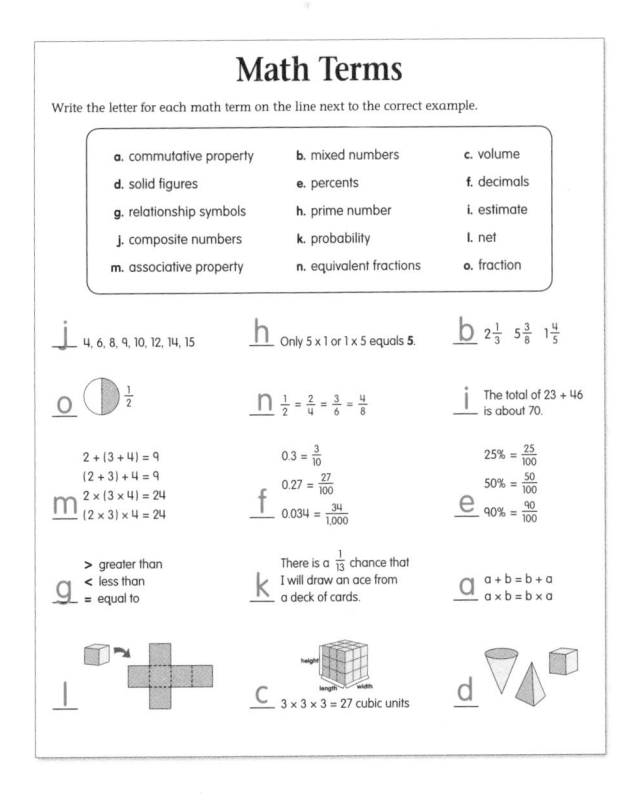

Math Terms

Write the letter for each math term on the line next to the correct example.

a. commutative property	**b.** mixed numbers	**c.** volume
d. solid figures	**e.** percents	**f.** decimals
g. relationship symbols	**h.** prime number	**i.** estimate
j. composite numbers	**k.** probability	**l.** net
m. associative property	**n.** equivalent fractions	**o.** fraction

j 4, 6, 8, 9, 10, 12, 14, 15

h Only 5 x 1 or 1 x 5 equals **5**.

b $2\frac{1}{3}$ $5\frac{3}{8}$ $1\frac{4}{5}$

o $\frac{1}{2}$

n $\frac{1}{2} = \frac{2}{4} = \frac{3}{6} = \frac{4}{8}$

i The total of 23 + 46 is about 70.

m
$2 + (3 + 4) = 9$
$(2 + 3) + 4 = 9$
$2 \times (3 \times 4) = 24$
$(2 \times 3) \times 4 = 24$

f
$0.3 = \frac{3}{10}$
$0.27 = \frac{27}{100}$
$0.034 = \frac{34}{1,000}$

e
$25\% = \frac{25}{100}$
$50\% = \frac{50}{100}$
$90\% = \frac{90}{100}$

g
$>$ greater than
$<$ less than
$=$ equal to

k There is a $\frac{1}{3}$ chance that I will draw an ace from a deck of cards.

a
$a + b = b + a$
$a \times b = b \times a$

l

c $3 \times 3 \times 3 = 27$ cubic units

d

Take It to Your Seat Centers—Math • EMC 3075 • © Evan-Moor Corp.

Math Terms

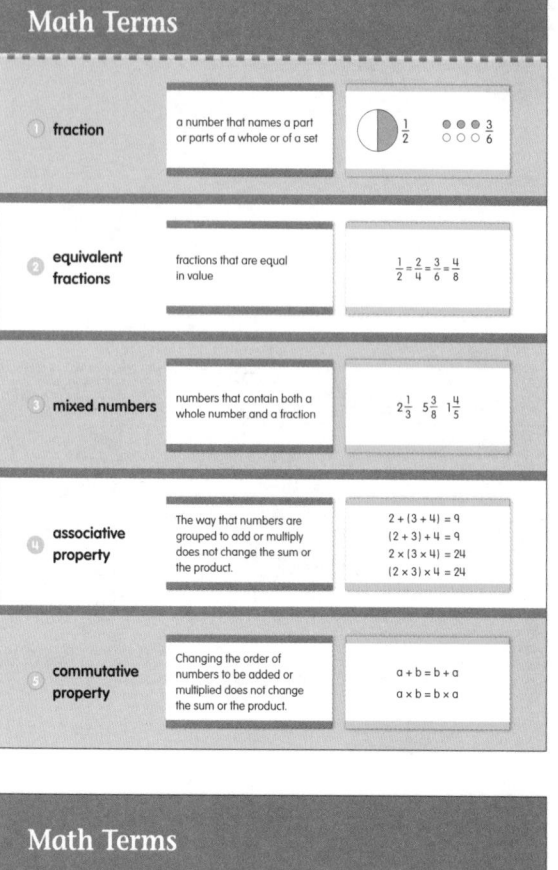

Math Terms

1. **fraction** — a number that names a part or parts of a whole or of a set
   $\frac{1}{2}$ $\frac{3}{6}$

2. **equivalent fractions** — fractions that are equal in value
   $\frac{1}{2} = \frac{2}{4} = \frac{3}{6} = \frac{4}{8}$

3. **mixed numbers** — numbers that contain both a whole number and a fraction
   $2\frac{1}{3}$ $5\frac{3}{8}$ $1\frac{4}{5}$

4. **associative property** — The way that numbers are grouped to add or multiply does not change the sum or the product.
   $2 + (3 + 4) = 9$
   $(2 + 3) + 4 = 9$
   $2 \times (3 \times 4) = 24$
   $(2 \times 3) \times 4 = 24$

5. **commutative property** — Changing the order of numbers to be added or multiplied does not change the sum or the product.
   $a + b = b + a$
   $a \times b = b \times a$

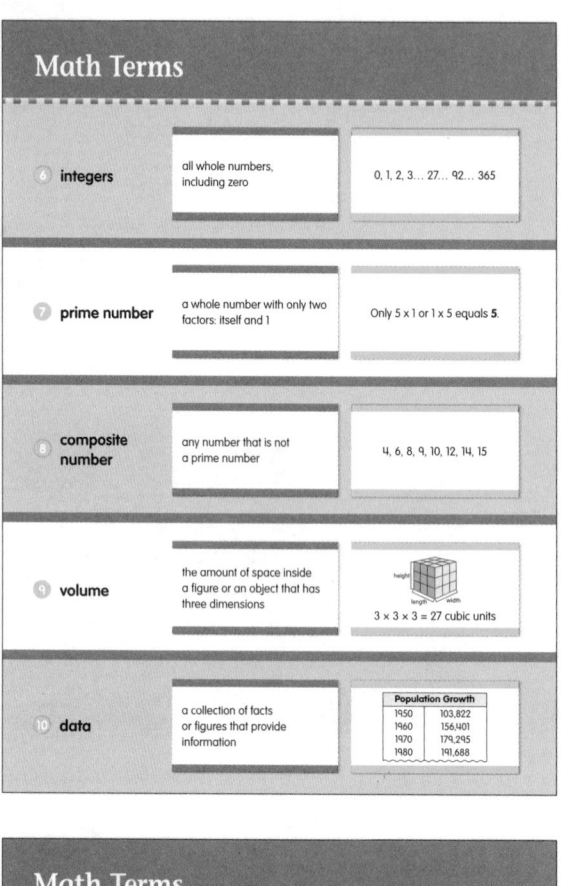

Math Terms

6. **integers** — all whole numbers, including zero
   0, 1, 2, 3... 27... 92... 365

7. **prime number** — a whole number with only two factors: itself and 1
   Only 5 x 1 or 1 x 5 equals **5**.

8. **composite number** — any number that is not a prime number
   4, 6, 8, 9, 10, 12, 14, 15

9. **volume** — the amount of space inside a figure or an object that has three dimensions
   $3 \times 3 \times 3 = 27$ cubic units

10. **data** — a collection of facts or figures that provide information

Population Growth	
1950	103,822
1960	156,401
1970	179,295
1980	191,688

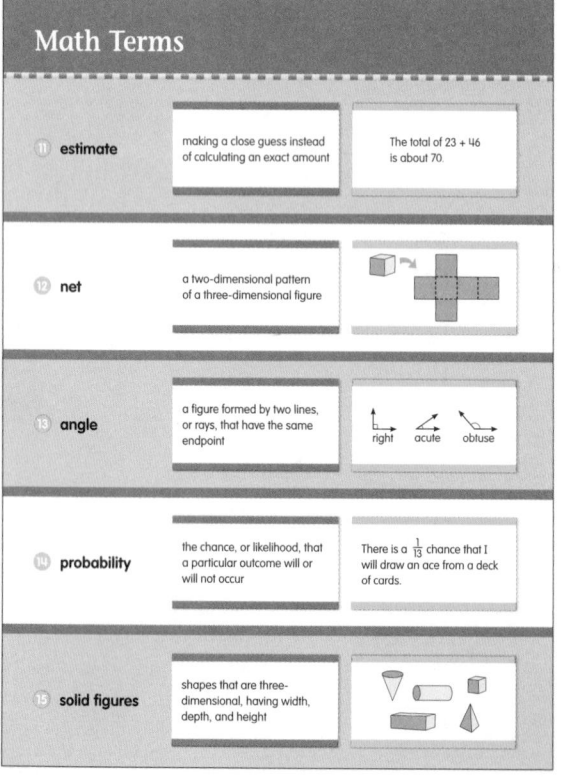

Math Terms

11. **estimate** — making a close guess instead of calculating an exact amount
    The total of 23 + 46 is about 70.

12. **net** — a two-dimensional pattern of a three-dimensional figure

13. **angle** — a figure formed by two lines, or rays, that have the same endpoint
    right acute obtuse

14. **probability** — the chance, or likelihood, that a particular outcome will or will not occur
    There is a $\frac{1}{13}$ chance that I will draw an ace from a deck of cards.

15. **solid figures** — shapes that are three-dimensional, having width, depth, and height

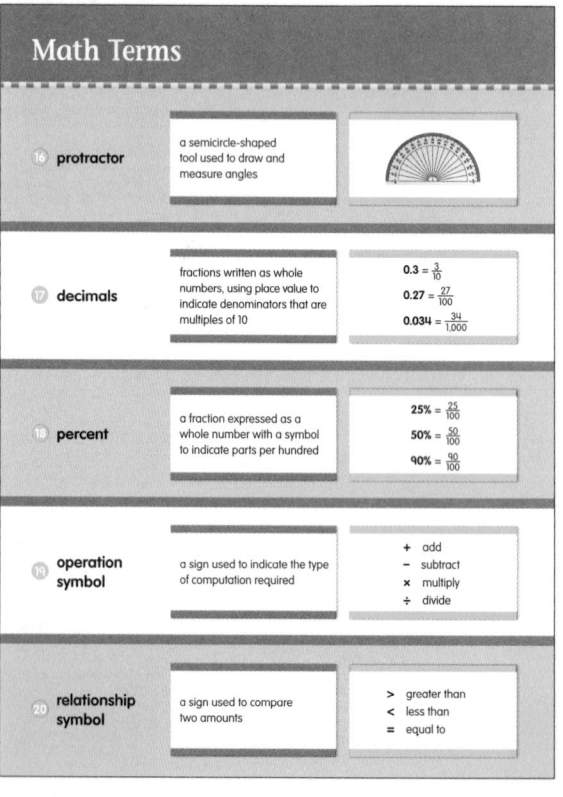

Math Terms

16. **protractor** — a semicircle-shaped tool used to draw and measure angles

17. **decimals** — fractions written as whole numbers, using place value to indicate denominators that are multiples of 10
    $0.3 = \frac{3}{10}$
    $0.27 = \frac{27}{100}$
    $0.034 = \frac{34}{1,000}$

18. **percent** — a fraction expressed as a whole number with a symbol to indicate parts per hundred
    $25\% = \frac{25}{100}$
    $50\% = \frac{50}{100}$
    $90\% = \frac{90}{100}$

19. **operation symbol** — a sign used to indicate the type of computation required
    + add
    − subtract
    × multiply
    ÷ divide

20. **relationship symbol** — a sign used to compare two amounts
    > greater than
    < less than
    = equal to

Math Terms

1. **fraction** | definition | example

2. **equivalent fractions** | definition | example

3. **mixed numbers** | definition | example

4. **associative property** | definition | example

5. **commutative property** | definition | example

Take It to Your Seat Centers—Math • EMC 3075 • © Evan-Moor Corp.

Math Terms

6 integers

definition example

7 prime number

definition example

8 composite number

definition example

9 volume

definition example

10 data

definition example

Math Terms

11 estimate

| definition | example |

12 net

| definition | example |

13 angle

| definition | example |

14 probability

| definition | example |

15 solid figures

| definition | example |

Math Terms

16 protractor | definition | example

17 decimals | definition | example

18 percent | definition | example

19 operation symbol | definition | example

20 relationship symbol | definition | example

all whole numbers, including zero	a whole number with only two factors: itself and 1	any number that is not a prime number
a collection of facts or figures that provide information	the amount of space inside a figure or an object that has three dimensions	a number that names a part or parts of a whole or of a set
fractions that are equal in value	numbers that contain both a whole number and a fraction	The way that numbers are grouped to add or multiply does not change the sum or the product.
Changing the order of numbers to be added or multiplied does not change the sum or the product.	making a close guess instead of calculating an exact amount	a two-dimensional pattern of a three-dimensional figure
a figure formed by two lines, or rays, that have the same endpoint	the chance, or likelihood, that a particular outcome will or will not occur	shapes that are three-dimensional, having width, depth, and height
a semicircle-shaped tool used to draw and measure angles	fractions written as whole numbers, using place value to indicate denominators that are multiples of 10	a fraction expressed as a whole number with a symbol to indicate parts per hundred
a sign used to indicate the type of computation required	a sign used to compare two amounts	

Math Terms

EMC 3075

© Evan-Moor Corp.

Math Terms

EMC 3075

© Evan-Moor Corp.

Math Terms

EMC 3075

© Evan-Moor Corp.

Math Terms

EMC 3075

© Evan-Moor Corp.

Math Terms

EMC 3075

© Evan-Moor Corp.

Math Terms

EMC 3075

© Evan-Moor Corp.

Math Terms

EMC 3075

© Evan-Moor Corp.

Math Terms

EMC 3075

© Evan-Moor Corp.

Math Terms

EMC 3075

© Evan-Moor Corp.

Math Terms

EMC 3075

© Evan-Moor Corp.

Math Terms

EMC 3075

© Evan-Moor Corp.

Math Terms

EMC 3075

© Evan-Moor Corp.

Math Terms

EMC 3075

© Evan-Moor Corp.

Math Terms

EMC 3075

© Evan-Moor Corp.

Math Terms

EMC 3075

© Evan-Moor Corp.

Math Terms

EMC 3075

© Evan-Moor Corp.

Math Terms

EMC 3075

© Evan-Moor Corp.

Math Terms

EMC 3075

© Evan-Moor Corp.

Math Terms

EMC 3075

© Evan-Moor Corp.

Math Terms

EMC 3075

© Evan-Moor Corp.

| 0, 1, 2, 3... 27... 92... 365 | Only 5 x 1 or 1 x 5 equals **5**. | 4, 6, 8, 9, 10, 12, 14, 15 |

Population Growth		
1950	103,822	
1960	156,401	
1970	179,295	
1980	191,688	

$3 \times 3 \times 3 = 27$ cubic units

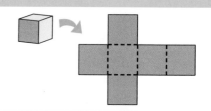

$\frac{1}{2}$ 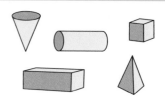 $\frac{3}{6}$

$\frac{1}{2} = \frac{2}{4} = \frac{3}{6} = \frac{4}{8}$

$2\frac{1}{3}$ $5\frac{3}{8}$ $1\frac{4}{5}$

$2 + (3 + 4) = 9$
$(2 + 3) + 4 = 9$
$2 \times (3 \times 4) = 24$
$(2 \times 3) \times 4 = 24$

$a + b = b + a$
$a \times b = b \times a$

The total of $23 + 46$ is about 70.

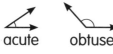
right   acute   obtuse

There is a $\frac{1}{13}$ chance that I will draw an ace from a deck of cards.

$0.3 = \frac{3}{10}$

$0.27 = \frac{27}{100}$

$0.034 = \frac{34}{1,000}$

$25\% = \frac{25}{100}$

$50\% = \frac{50}{100}$

$90\% = \frac{90}{100}$

+   add
−   subtract
×   multiply
÷   divide

>   greater than
<   less than
=   equal to

Math Terms

EMC 3075

© Evan-Moor Corp.

Math Terms

EMC 3075

© Evan-Moor Corp.

Math Terms

EMC 3075

© Evan-Moor Corp.

Math Terms

EMC 3075

© Evan-Moor Corp.

Math Terms

EMC 3075

© Evan-Moor Corp.

Math Terms

EMC 3075

© Evan-Moor Corp.

Math Terms

EMC 3075

© Evan-Moor Corp.

Math Terms

EMC 3075

© Evan-Moor Corp.

Math Terms

EMC 3075

© Evan-Moor Corp.

Math Terms

EMC 3075

© Evan-Moor Corp.

Math Terms

EMC 3075

© Evan-Moor Corp.

Math Terms

EMC 3075

© Evan-Moor Corp.

Math Terms

EMC 3075

© Evan-Moor Corp.

Math Terms

EMC 3075

© Evan-Moor Corp.

Math Terms

EMC 3075

© Evan-Moor Corp.

Math Terms

EMC 3075

© Evan-Moor Corp.

Math Terms

EMC 3075

© Evan-Moor Corp.

Math Terms

EMC 3075

© Evan-Moor Corp.

Literacy Centers

GRADES PreK–6

Add some creativity to your literacy practice with hanger pocket, shoe box, and folder centers! Each full-color literacy center uses a motivating theme and full-color materials to get your students involved in literacy practice! 192 full-color pages.

PreK–K*	EMC 2401	Grades 3–4	EMC 2124
Grades K–1	EMC 2123	Grades 4–5	EMC 2724
Grades 1–3	EMC 788	Grades 4–6	EMC 2719
Grades 2–3	EMC 2723		

*Includes language arts and math centers

Grade 2

Phonics Centers

GRADES PreK–3

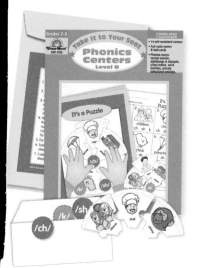

Hands-on phonics practice that students love! Fun, game-like formats and full-color task cards create the perfect tool to teach your students valuable phonics skills, such as rhyming words, initial and final consonant sounds, consonant blends, and more! 192 full-color pages.

PreK–K	Level A	EMC 3327
Grades K–1	Level B	EMC 3328
Grades 1–2	Level C	EMC 3329
Grades 2–3	Level D	EMC 3330

Phonics Games

Centers for Up to 6 Players

GRADES PreK–3

Each *Phonics Games* title covers the same skills as the corresponding *Basic Phonics Skills* book in a fun, hands-on format. Move through Levels A through D to sequentially practice phonics skills, beginning with phonemic awareness and ending with structural analysis, or pick the games that address your students' needs. The 7 colorful, engaging games inspire students at every level! 144 full-color pages.

Grades PreK–K	Level A	EMC 3362
Grades K–1	Level B	EMC 3363
Grades 1–2	Level C	EMC 3364
Grades 2–3	Level D	EMC 3365

Reading and Language Centers

GRADES K–6+

Engage your students in reading and language skills practice! The full-color centers in each ALL NEW *Take It to Your Seat Reading and Language Centers* title cover skills such as sequencing, predicting, distinguishing between real and make-believe, and more! 160 pages.

Grade K	EMC 2840		Grade 4	EMC 2844
Grade 1	EMC 2841		Grade 5	EMC 2845
Grade 2	EMC 2842		Grade 6+	EMC 2846
Grade 3	EMC 2843			

Centers

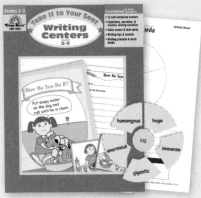

Grades 2–3

"I love that Take It to Your Seat Learning Centers have hands-on learning activities followed by a paper-and-pencil activity. They're simply the best!"

–Sandy O.
Second Grade Teacher

Writing Centers
GRADES 1–6

Help students practice writing strong sentences & paragraphs, stories & poems, notes & letters, and more! Writing tips, models, prompts, and word banks help guide students through the entire writing process. 192 full-color pages.

Grades 1–2 EMC 6002		**Grades 4–5** EMC 6005
Grades 2–3 EMC 6003		**Grades 5–6** EMC 6006
Grades 3–4 EMC 6004		

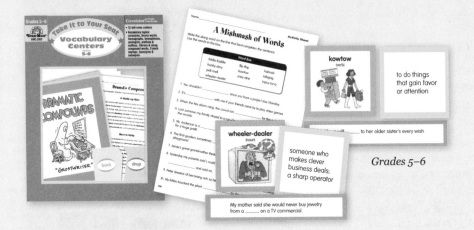

Grades 5–6

Vocabulary Centers
GRADES K–6

Engage your students as they build vocabulary and practice important skills such as analogies, prefixes and suffixes, synonyms, and more! 192 full-color pages.

Grades K–1 EMC 3347	**Grades 3–4** EMC 3350
Grades 1–2 EMC 3348	**Grades 4–5** EMC 3351
Grades 2–3 EMC 3349	**Grades 5–6** EMC 3352

Grades PreK–K

Science Centers
GRADES PreK–4

Science Centers cover grade-level science concepts. 192 full-color pages.

Grades PreK–K	EMC 5004
Grades 1–2	EMC 5002
Grades 3–4	EMC 5003

Grades 1–2

Geography Centers
GRADES 1–5

Help students practice geography vocabulary and concepts. 192 full-color pages.

Grades 1–2 EMC 3716	**Grades 3–4** EMC 3718
Grades 2–3 EMC 3717	**Grades 4–5** EMC 3719